Délie MULLER and Jean-Yves BOSCHER

Curators of the Musée d'Aquitaine

With the participation of A. and D. KUMURDJIAN

BORDEAUX

Photographs by André KURMUDJIAN

GRAND SUD Editions

Bordeaux

« Great ships, our burning love for you has been to no avail;
The very last among you has taken to the sea.
The setting sun has stolen so many in full sail
That ever more this port, my heart, an aching void shall be. »

(Jean de La Ville de Mirmont)

The town's façade looking over the Garonne

The Garonne, "the sea", as it was called in the Middle Ages: what has the river done to the port spoken of by the young poet, a friend of François Mauriac's, who died at the beginning of the First World War? In fact, it is quite the opposite. It was the ungrateful city that turned its back on the river that was its lifeblood.
The Bordelais, busy with his vines and his trading, was keen to own ships but not to take the helm. However much he imbued the sea with symbolism, the waves were merely the carrier of the riches of the land on which he had built his fortune. His need for harmonious stability combined with prestige is expressed in three centuries of architecture, the art form best suited to the temperament of the Bordelais.
Though tastes change with time, the façades of one century have never clashed with those of another. From the work of the Intendants to the great public buildings, from the great hôtels, the townhouses of the residential districts to the échoppes, the cottages of the Barrières, from the golden stone of yesteryear to contemporary concrete and glass, the visitor will find an incomparable townscape.

For centuries, great sailing ships plied up and down the estuary and the river, where nowadays only net fishermen work, perched on the end of piers scattered all along the banks of the Garonne.

With its short texts and its many illustrations, this guide turns a stroll around Bordeaux into an adventure of discovery.

You can follow the circular itineraries from their starting points or take them up at any other point. An index on the back page will help you locate streets and the main monuments on the foldaway plan inside the back cover.

Bus routes 7/8 and 1 have stops on the itineraries, and routes 3, 4, 5 and 6 cross several of them.
We have taken great care to provide concise information, resulting from the latest work carried out by our colleagues in the Heritage Department and by lecturers and researchers at the University. Thanks to their assistance and the bibliography at the back of the book, you will be able to satisfy your curiosity and increase your knowledge of the city.

A SHORT HISTORY OF BORDEAUX

Ancient Burdigala is thought to have been founded in the 3rd century BC by the Bituriges Vivisci, a Gaulish tribe which settled at the western end of the "isthmus of Gaul" (the shortest route from the Mediterranean to the Atlantic) close to the Gironde estuary at the confluence of the Devèze and the Garonne. From there, they could control the trade in tin from Armorica (Brittany) and the British Isles.

Stele dedicated to a young child by his father, Laetus. In the first century, in Gaul, cocks and cats were often children's pets.

The Bituriges rallied peacefully to Caesar. In the 1st to 3rd centuries AD, the first Roman town plan fixed the two main streets (the cardo and the decumanus) which became the rue Sainte-Catherine and the rue Porte-Dijeaux and have always been the city's most frequented streets.

The first vines were planted around Burdigala in about 50 AD. The effect of Romanization was to make the market town a cosmopolitan city, the administrative capital of Aquitania, a meeting place for people from all over the Empire - Iberians, Jews, Greeks, Treviri, Britons and many others. Important public monuments were built, such as the Palace of Gallienus and the Pillars of Tutellus, before the city closed itself in behind its ramparts after the first barbarian invasions in around 276 AD.

In the 4th century, at the time of Paulinus of Nola and the poet Ausonius (310-394), the city's university and intellectual life spread its fame across the Roman world. At the same time, Christianity reached the city, which became the seat of the diocese of Aquitaine, and a pilgrims' road was created between Bordeaux and Jerusalem (333).

In 409, the Vandals pillaged the city. Euric, King of the Visigoths who had settled here in 418, made Bordeaux his capital in 475. The Frankish period followed, then the time of the Gascon Dukes. Loup, Eudes and Waïfre tried in vain to resist the pressure of Charles the Hammer and Pepin the Short. With the arrival of Charlemagne, the city came under the authority of the Carolingian Counts.

In 848, the Vikings sacked and burned the city, sounding the death-knell of what remained of Burdigala and its Gallo-Roman civilization. At the end of the 10th century, the County of Bordeaux passed into the hands of the Dukes of Gascony, then to the Counts of Poitiers who became the Dukes of Aquitaine in 1058, lords of a dukedom that stretched from the Loire to the Pyrenees. In 1137 in St. André's Cathedral, their heiress, Eleanor of Aquitaine, married the future Louis VII, King of France. Fifteen years later, she became the wife of Henry Plantagenet who, on becoming King of England in 1154, brought Bordeaux under English control for 300 years.

Stained glass window showing the arms of Bordeaux (15th century) from St Seurin's Basilica : the Crescent Moon (symbolising the form of the Garonne as it passes the town : "Port de la Lune" (moon)), the Grosse Cloche (town belfry in the Middle Ages) and the three English leopards (reduced to one since 1453).

Bird's-eye view of Bordeaux which appeared in the Cosmography of Munster and Belleforest in 1575. Visible in the town enclosed within its ramparts are the Gallo-Roman remains of the Pillars of Tutellus (destroyed in 1677 by Louis XIV to extend the glacis of Château Trompette), the Fort du Hâ, St André, Porte Cailhau etc. At the top right is Palace of Gallienus.

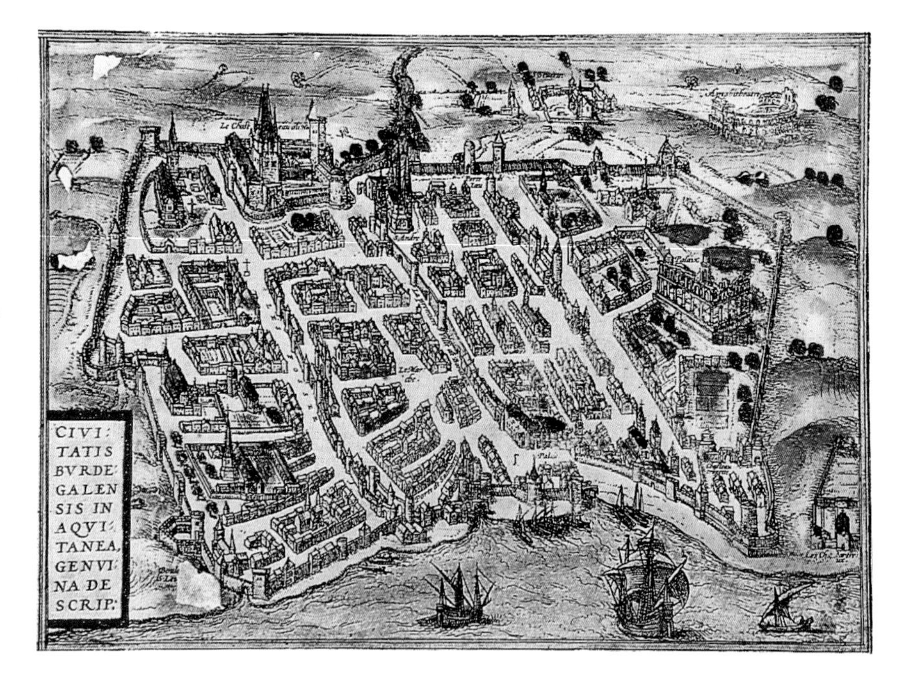

The 12th century marked a revival in the city's fortunes. Outside the walls, a market - Lou Mercat - was set up in 1155, around which arose the Faubourg St. Eloi, soon protected by a new double wall completed in 1227. It was perhaps at the time of the siege of St. Eloi by Alfonso VII of Castile in 1206 that the Bordelais, encouraged by the freedoms granted to them by Eleanor and her son John Lackland in 1199, set themselves up as a self-governing community. Rival families - the Solers, Coloms, Monadeys, Caillaus and others - vied for control of the city government, the Jurade (1249-1310). The King-Duke took advantage of the dispute to make himself mayor in 1325.

In the same period, the vines, which had been maintained by the clergy, began to spread and kept spreading. Wine produced over 95% of all Bordeaux's trade profits, with a further boost in October 1225 when the city was given exclusive rights to ship its harvests to England. It was a new golden age for the city, reaching its apogee in 1307 with a tonnage that was only beaten in 1950! The King of England had a hand in it too, by protecting and chartering large convoys. It has often been said that Bordeaux's wine was at the root of England's maritime might!
Surrounded by convents, the city had grown. The last new walls were built between 1302 and 1327.
From 1362 to 1372, the Black Prince held sumptuous court in Bordeaux, and like his father Edward III, he minted prestige gold coins.
After the defeat and death of the English General Talbot at Castillon-la-Bataille, the Hundred Years' War ended in October 1453 with the capitulation of Bordeaux, which was still pro-English, bringing three centuries of English presence to a close.
The Fort du Hâ and the first Château Trompette were then built to defend the city against foreign incursions, and Bordeaux was given a Parliament in 1462.
All through the 16th and 17th centuries, the city put up strong resistance against the centralist monarchy; there were revolts, as in 1548 against the gabelle, the salt tax, in 1635 against the wine tax, in 1648 with the Ormée insurrection - Bordeaux's part in the Fronde, the uprising against Mazarin - and lastly in 1675, the last throes of a proud city which finally bowed to the power of the King and his Intendants.
Bordeaux became an important centre for humanism in 1533 with the founding of the Collège de Guyenne, where many foreign academics came to teach, many of them fleeing the Reformation. Another teacher was Elie Vinet, Bordeaux's first historiographer. Montaigne studied there. The Parliament became a breeding ground for writers, poets and thinkers, one of the most brilliant being Montaigne's great friend La Boétie.
The Parliament condemned the Reformation, repressing it severely in 1538. Bordeaux, as elsewhere in France, had its St. Bartholomew's Day massacre of Protestants in August 1572. Montaigne (1533-1592), mayor from 1581 to 1585 and a wise administrator, protected the city from the Leaguers and played the role of intermediary between the governor and the future Henry IV, whose ascension to the throne he foresaw.
In the early 17th century under François de Sourdis, Bordeaux became an important centre of the Counter-Reformation. New religious orders moved to the city, such as the Feuillants, the Ursulines, the Visitandines and the Carmelites.
The Ormée uprising in 1651-53 sketched the outline of a innovative form of government and a republican spirit. The beaten Bordelais watched as a more imposing second Château Trompette was built. To extend the glacis, the King had the Pillars of Tutellus (les Piliers de Tutelle) demolished, along with the entire district between the fort and the city. At the other end of town, he built Fort Louis.
Once the people settled down again, another age dawned with the founding of the Chamber of Commerce in 1705, which brought unprecedented growth in trade. A shipbuilding and fitting industry was set up, so too was the triangular trade route between Bordeaux, Africa and the West Indies, as planned by Colbert. On the eve of the Revolution, Bordeaux was the greatest port in France.

Bust of Cardinal François de Sourdis, archbishop of Bordeaux from 1599 to 1628, by le Bernin. The most important figure in the town, he was also a shrewd patron of the arts.

The Intendants Boucher and Tourny transformed the city and made it beautiful, while Dupré de St. Maur completed the drainage system. The city opened up, after fourteen centuries behind its walls. A new intellectual life flourished with the founding of the Academy and the presence of Montesquieu, author of "L'Esprit des Lois", the basis of the future constitution of the United States and of the ideology of the Revolution.

Bust of Montesquieu by J. B. Lemoyne

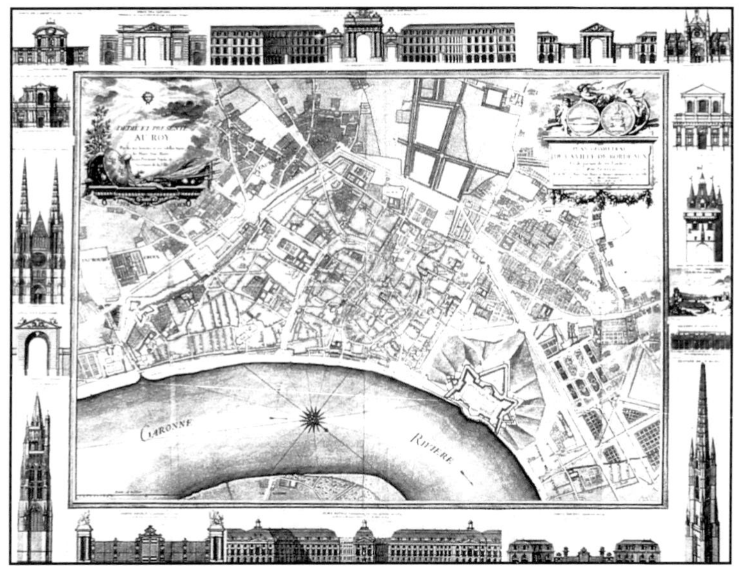

Plan of Bordeaux drawn by Lattré in 1754 showing the main buildings of the town and the recent works of the Intendants : demolition of the ramparts, rectilinear layout of the principal roads, the façade overlooking the river, promenades and gardens.

During the Revolution, the Bordelais and the Girondins, members of the well-off, thinking class of lawyers, doctors, and merchants, all defending liberal ideas, heeded the call of Vergniaud in 1793 and tried to rebel against the Jacobin centralism of Paris, with hopes of a federalist system. During the Terror, Thérésia Cabarrus, the famous Mme Tallien, intervened many times to save a number of citizens from the guillotine.
Severely affected by the years of revolution and the Continental Block during the First Empire, Bordeaux's trade took off again under the Restoration. The city, which had allied itself with the Bourbons on 12 March 1814, retained its 18th century heritage and the city's mayors continued the transformation work.
The Pont de Pierre, completed in 1822, finally linked the two banks of the Garonne. The city became an important place for trade guilds, welcomed the railways (Bordeaux - La Teste in 1837, Paris - Bordeaux in 1852), restarted shipbuilding and became the major port of embarkation for South America, Morocco and the colonies in Black Africa and Oceania.

Bordeaux's boats had fished for cod off Newfoundland since 1517, and towards the end of the 19th century, this activity and deep sea fishing for other species experienced a boom, in a port which at last had vertical wharves (from about 1840) and a wet dock. On the right bank, the Queyries landing stages were built in 1890, and the Bastide district continued to spread out from the end of the Pont de Pierre. The docks with their mechanical cranes were already moving downstream towards the Chartrons and Bacalan.
In the dark hours of war, in 1870 when Gambetta gave his famous speech, then in 1914 and 1940, the National Assembly and the Government made their headquarters in Bordeaux for a time. The inter-war years were marked by major building projects (the stadium, swimming pool, Labour Exchange, etc) initiated by mayor Adrien Marquet and his architect Jacques d'Welles, and by the last great period of port traffic, when liners and freighters endlessly plied the river. An early bid to give the city modern, modular architecture, the Cité Frugès in Pessac, designed by Le Corbusier (1927), did not win favour and was rejected. After 1945, efforts were directed into building programmes aimed at solving the housing crisis and, a new move, towards the industrialization that the city had so long refused. All this was done at the instance of the young mayor, Jacques Chaban Delmas. The dilapidated Mériadeck district was razed and completely remodelled, and a huge complex was built at Bordeaux-Lac for staging major regional and international exhibitions, while in the suburbs, new businesses set up, developing state-of-the-art technology. The port has moved to Le Verdon in order to deal with containers and large tankers, and the city has reclaimed its creamy façades in the most extensive urban conservation area in France. On the eve of the third millennium, ambitious development plans have been announced for the right bank.
Bordeaux has been modernised in the 21st century : work on both banks of the river has largely cleared the quays of boathouses and cars, leaving space for city life and pedestrians. On the left bank, 30 hectares for use of the public have been created and the rehabilitation of several boathouses on the edge of the Garonne river has been completed. Nowadays, the city has a tramway, work has been done to improve the city's squares and other areas have been modernised. This has contributed to the overall embellishment of the environment, giving a fresh impetus to the pleasure of living in the city.

The large bay of the Hôtel de Region, on the right scanned with "blades" of stone. The interplay of the metal structure (in places for effect only) with glass and the emergency stairway highlighted as an element of the design are typical ot the new "Mériadeck district" which has replaced the old insalubrious buildings built on the drained marsh.

The Crown Court (1994-1998), the work of the architect Richard Rogers.

The great planners, architects and sculptors in Bordeaux

Abadie, Paul (1812-1884), diocesan architect (Sacré-Coeur in Paris, St. Front in Périgueux). Bordeaux: St. André, St. Seurin, St. Michel, Ste. Croix, Ste. Marie.

Bonfin, Richard (1730-1814), city architect in 1751: Palais Rohan, Hôtel de Lisleferme, La Grave fountain and many houses.

Boucher, Claude (1673-1752), Intendant of Guyenne 1720-1743: instigator of the Place de la Bourse, a breach in the medieval ramparts.

Burguet, Jean (1783-1848), neoclassical architect: St. André's Hospital, south side of the Pavé des Chartrons, hemicycle of Place des Quinconces.

Cabirol, Barthélémy (1732-1786) Bordeaux sculptor and ornamentalist: rooms in the Hôtel de la Bourse, Palais Rohan, Hôtel de Lisleferme, etc

Combes, Louis (1757-1818), architect: Hôtel Acquart, Hôtel Meyer, Dépôt de Mendicité, Château Margaux, etc

Deschamps, Claude (1765-1843), civil engineer: Pont de Pierre, Entrepôts Lainé, Libourne bridge

Dufart, Jean-Baptiste (1752-1818), Louis' designer then architect: Hôtel Fenwick, Théâtre Français, houses on Place des Quinconces, Châteaux in the Bordelais (Beauséjour, Burk), etc.

Dumilâtre (1844-1927), designer, and Debrie, Gustave (1853-1924), sculptor of the Monument to the Girondins.

Duplessis, Pierre-Michel (1633-1693), architect-engineer: Notre-Dame church, Bordeaux townhouses ("hôtels"), work on the Château Trompette, Fort Paté, Fort Médoc, etc.

Dupré de Saint-Maur, Nicolas (1732-1791), Intendant of Guyenne 1776-85: completed the draining of the marshes in the city.

Francin, Claude (1702-1773), sculptor at the royal workshops: ornamentation on doors, pediments and the pedestal of the statue of Louis XV (Place de la Bourse), the portico of the Riding School, etc

Gabriel, Jacques (1667-1742) and Jacques-Ange (1698-1782), architects. Jacques, the King's architect, was responsible for the Place Royale (Pl. de la Bourse), completed by his son Jacques-Ange, who also built the Gabriel wing at Versailles, the Petit Trianon, the Château de Compiègne, the Ecole Militaire in Paris, etc.

Laclotte, Etienne (1734-1812), architect from a Bordeaux dynasty: sections of the Faubourg Saint-Seurin, the Capuchins convent, the Hôtel de Lalande, houses in rue Huguerie and rue Victoire Américaine, the Hôtels Bonaffé, Labottière, etc.

Lhote, François (1750-1808), architect: Hôtel Journu, section of rue Huguerie and rue Rolland, Hôtel Piganeau

Louis, Louis-Nicolas, Victor (1731-1800), architect: Grand Theatre, townhouses in the Ilot Louis (Hôtels Saige, Legrix, Boyer-Fonfrède, La Molère), Hôtel Rolly, Hôtel Nairac, Château du Bouilh, etc. Elsewhere: The Royal Palace in Warsaw, the Comédie Française and pavilions at the Palais Royal in Paris, etc

Maggesi, Dominique (1802-1892), official city sculptor: many busts, statues, and tombs of great figures and local personalities throughout the city.

Portier, André (1702-1770), architect to Intendant Tourny: Allées de Tourny, Porte-Dijeaux, Porte d'Aquitaine, Porte des Salinières, gate of the Riding School, Hôtel de la Tresne, Hôtel Perrier de Larsan, etc

Prévot, Edmond (1848-1892) and Coeffard de Mazerolles, Louis (1818-1877), sculptors: front of the Town Hall, west front of St. Seurin (Prévot), the nymph in the Audège fountain (Mazerolles)

Richelieu, Louis-Armand Duplessis, Duc de (1696-1788), governor of Guyenne from 1758, he was behind the building of the Grand Theatre. He was the great-nephew of the famous Cardinal.

Tourny, Louis Aubert de (1695-1760), Intendant of Guyenne 1743-57: completed the Place Royale (Pl. de la Bourse) and designed Bordeaux's riverside frontage, the rectangular courtyards, squares and gates of the 18th century city.

Welles, Jacques Boistel d' (1883-1970), city architect in the inter-war period: stadium, Labour Exchange (Bourse du Travail), terraces and stands in the Jardin Public (restoration work).

From Saint-Seurin to Saint-Bruno

Leaving the Cours du XXX Juillet, walk up the Cours de l'Intendance past the smartest shops in the "Triangle" to Place Gambetta. From there, go to Place des Martyrs de la Résistance by taking rue Judaïque, which was outside the walls in medieval times. There stands the ancient collegiate church (i.e. "church of the canons") of St. Seurin, from the name of the Byzantine prelate who is said to have been bishop in the early 5th century. In the 4th century, the Christian converts settled on the site of a great Gallo-Roman necropolis, which they too used for burials. Close by at St. Etienne stood the first cathedral, only a small church, demolished in 1787. The bishop's throne was transferred inside the ramparts in the 6th century.

In the 20th century, excavations have uncovered two burial complexes. The decoration (frescoes, chrisma, etc), tombs (earth, tiles, amphorae, marble sarcophagi) and objects found inside (flasks, ceramics, coins) have proved to be an invaluable source of information about the early chapters of Christian history in Bordeaux. The entrance to the Palaeochristian site, run by the Tourist Office, is in the garden near the South door of the church.

St Seurin's Basilica : the Romanesque bell tower is separate from the rear of the west façade built in 1829, where, as dictated by tradition, the actual entrance to the church is situated (C). The church is listed as world heritage as part of the Saint Jacques de Compostelle pilgrim paths.

The story of the church begins in the crypt, which was first the baptistery, then the necropolis, where the bones of bishops St. Amand and St. Seurin lie. The veneration of the two saints made the church a basilica, a monastery, and Bordeaux's great sanctuary, considered as the "equal" of the cathedral. The lay canons who, from the 12th century, ruled over an extensive domain, tried to make the most of their privileges by attracting pilgrims to the relics of the founding "saints" and "inventing" the veneration of St. Fort. It was also said that St. Martial had left St. Peter's staff there, and that Charlemagne had left Roland's horn! With the cathedral they shared the right to baptize. The Dukes and Counts were invested there, and the future archbishops spent the night before entering Bordeaux on the "throne" in the basilica. This helps us better understand the history of the construction of the church and its fittings: the Romanesque church was built around the crypt and was itself enveloped in the Gothic construction which was remodelled in the 19th century! Side chapels were added later.
On the south front the old entrance to the basilica hides under a Renaissance porch. Following Romanesque tradition in the South West, the usual three doors of the great fronts of cathedrals here become one "real" door between two "blind" ones, which still however retain their tympana and statues. The trefoil-arched lintel is decorated with vine leaves which remind us of the ones on the sarcophagi in the crypt. On the tympanum, the Last Judgement and the decor recall the Royal Door at St. André's Cathedral.

Romanesque capital (E) depicting the sacrifice of Abraham, one of the most popular scenes of the time, relating 'symbolically' with the sacrifice of Christ.

South Door : the Synagogue with its oriental style tympanum (B).

Standing under Romanesque-type architecture (around 1200 AD), the holy women at the tomb on the left and what may be a Resurrection scene on the right have the same decor of angels and Jews with their caps and phylacteries. The Twelve Apostles, the Church (A) and the Synagogue (B) on the stylobate are in full Gothic style. The West front (C) has statues of St. Seurin and St. Amand in two niches. Unfinished at the time of building, it was completed by Poitevin in Neoromanesque style in 1829.
Along the barrel-vaulted passage through the porch, two series of 12th century Romanesque capitals adorn the columns. High up on the right (D), a dead St. Seurin is laid out on an altar.

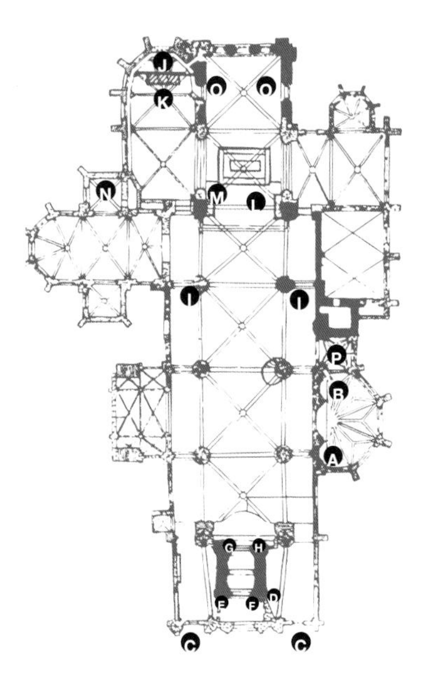

On the left (E) Abraham's sacrifice, and opposite, on the right, a set of animals (F) followed by four capitals with fabled animals, on the model of those found in Irish manuscripts or on Carolingian ivory carvings (G and H).
Going into the church, we see the reinforced pillars put in after the roof collapsed in 1698. The very wide nave is continued by the flat-apsed chancel in which there are three bays with plain capitals. The organ chest was the work of Cabirol in the 18th century. Note near the chancel the capitals with projecting faces (I) from the transitional period between Romanesque and Gothic. The great vault ribs, fanning out from the pillars and buttressed by side aisles with transverse barrel vaults, are unique in the Bordelais.
In the Sacred Heart chapel (N) on the right, a limestone St. Martial (around 1500), holding a staff, blesses the crowd. In St. Stephen's chapel (P) another St. Martial with finely chiselled clothing but a less expressive face reflects the spirit of "détente" of those times.
In the Flamboyant-style chapel of Our Lady of the Rose, an alabaster wall statue (J) with a Gothic slouch and a long face, carrying the Child on her left arm - contrary to custom - recalls the English Virgins of the 14th century. The twelve English alabaster panels on the life of the Blessed Virgin (K) were put back on the altar in the wrong order in the 19th century.
In the chancel are fourteen panels which, except for a Crucifixion and an Annunciation, tell the life stories of St. Martial and St. Seurin; the fine craftsmanship and iconography make us wonder whether there was a workshop in Bordeaux that worked in the same way as the alabastermen.

A set of alabaster panels recounting the life of St Martial and St Seurin

The detailed gothic decor of this stone cathedral, undoubtedly commissioned by Pey-Berland in the 15th century, is typified by the episcopal throne in wood. All future archbishops, in memory of their venerable predecessors, since the 6th century had to spend the night before their triumphal entry into the town and ordination in this throne.

Detail of a misericord: the grilling of a tongue

A relic of the days when the cathedral was in this district is the 15th century stone chair (M) on which the archbishop sat on the eve of his induction. Take time to admire the grotesque and amusing scenes on the misericords in the stalls (O).

The crypt, which has constantly been refashioned since the 4th century, is made up of elements ranging from a Gallo-Roman column, some lovely Merovingian marble sarcophagi, and Carolingian chancel plates set in the walls to a 12th century reliquary. The recently discovered square vat could have belonged to the old baptistery which preceded the very first church. For many years, children were brought here to be "fortified" by being presented to the makebelieve St. Fort in the apse.

The tomb of St Fort in the crypt : trditionally, children were 'fortified' through contact of the forehead with the stone of the tomb.

Merovingian sarcophagus

At n. 63, the greatly cultured merchant and refiner Frugès had a house built between 1913 and 1927. He wanted to create a fusion of Oriental and French art without neglecting local traditions. The result is a house in full art deco style; more than twenty artists and craftsmen were involved in the decoration and furnishing. Despite his eclectic tastes, the front elevation is conventional,

but the features have been given the full art deco treatment: the supports of the balconies, the loggia and the rotunda are decorated with vines (we are in Bordeaux, after all !). On the top storey on the rotunda wall, the gymnasts are a reminder of the gymnasium that lay behind the loggia.
Walk to St. Bruno's church. You can make a detour via **rue Judaïque**:
- rue d'Alzon, the arcaded front of the former Alhambra, dating from the 19th century.
- at n.166, rue Judaïque was the Riding School (Ecole d'Equitation et de dressage du Jardin Public) built in 1755 and transferred in 1856. It is now the entrance to the swimming pool. "Apollo in his chariot" on the pediment is by Francin.

Façade of the Frugès house : the rotunda.

Façade of the old Alhambra Theatre

St. Bruno's church, built between 1611 and 1620, is the former chapel of the second Carthusian convent, the gift of Blaise de Gascq (Brother Ambrose in religion) and the dream of Cardinal François de Sourdis, Archbishop of Bordeaux 1599-1628. It was built on former marshland on which drainage work had started in 1609 in the interests of public health. The site had many drainage canals, along which, over a large area at the side of the convent, pleasant walks were laid out. All that remains of the convent, demolished in the 19th century, is the church and the Porte de la Chartreuse (the gate on the northern side of the cemetery). St. Bruno's is the sole example of Roman Baroque art in the area, directly imported after trips to Rome by the ostentatious Bordeaux prelate and patron of the arts.
Dedicated to St. Bruno, according to the wishes of Blaise de Gascq, it was consecrated to Our Lady of Mercy on the initiative of François de Sourdis, full of Marian piety, as is recalled by the 1619 Latin inscription on the front, to the glory of the Blessed Virgin and the Cardinal.

The Baroque façade

The narrow front has three levels. It is scanned by a succession of pilasters, Corinthian at the torus, with plain shafts and consoles at the top, with alternating scroll and flame ornaments. A curved pediment tops the building, with a cartouche on the upper part on which can be seen the arms of Cardinal de Sourdis. In a niche, a Virgin and Child contrasts with the purity of line of the architecture. This very sober façade is linked by side walls (with tiered door, niche and pyramid) to two doors, one on the right in the mannerist style, opening onto the Carthusian convent, the other on the left, a 19th century copy, put in for symmetry.
Inside, a single barrel-vaulted nave is decorated with trompe-l'oeil vistas painted by Berinzago (18th century), now, alas, very worn. On the sides, part of the stalls by Elie Etier (around 1619) are still in place (A and B). Among the paintings, there is a life of St. Bruno, after Le Sueur (C), St. Sebastian (D), St. Jerome and the lion (E) with a Caravaggian flavour and St. Bruno in ecstasy (F).

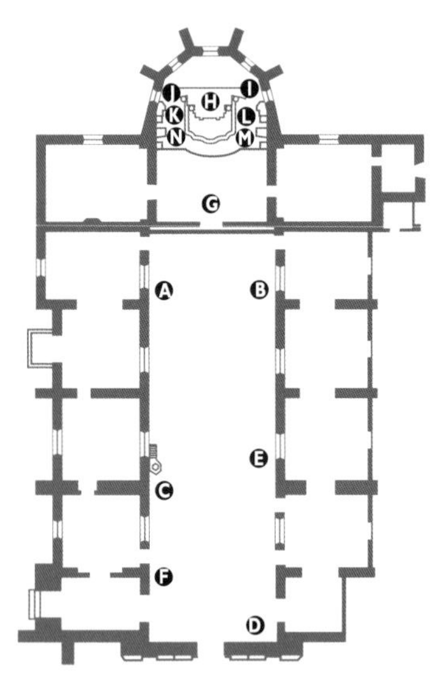

The chancel of St Bruno's Church

The outstanding choir (G) has a marble and Taillebourg stone decor, with alternating pilasters, niches and festoons crowned by a balustrade decorated with flame ornaments, all converging on the imposing marble columned reredos. At the back, either side of the Assumption (H) by Philippe de Champaigne (1673), the remarkable group of the Annunciation by the Berninis (around 1620): the Virgin (I), showing mannerist influence with its fine, pleated drape, is attributed to Pietro, while the Angel (J) with its supple movement and beautiful, serious face, is the work of his son Gian Lorenzo, famous in France as Le Cavalier Bernin. Facing each other in their niches, St. John the Baptist (K) and St. Joseph (L) were made by Bordeaux sculptor Jean Girouard around 1670-1675. His St. John is clearly inspired by Michelangelo. In the foreground are the sensitive works of the Florentine Ottaviano Lazeri (1620), probably commissioned by Cardinal de Sourdis during his last trip to Italy: St. Bruno (M), founder of the Carthusian order, wearing his sackcloth, and St. Charles Borromeo (N), reminding us of the important part played by the saint in applying the Tridentine reforms. The Cardinal saw himself as a disciple of St. Charles and held him in great veneration. The inspired face of the preacher, the care taken with the drape and the elegance of the pose make it a first class piece of sculpture.

The Blessed Virgin (I) by Pietro Bernini

Statue of St Charles Borromée (N) by Lazeri

Detail of the stalls of Elie Etier

The Carthusian cemetery

Marmiche Tomb : this chapel with a doric feel and perfectly proportioned is the masterpiece of this site. On the façade, Faith, framing the door, Despair and Eternal Sadness.

Opposite the church, on the site of the former walled area of the convent, we enter the graveyard known as the Cimetière de la Chartreuse, Bordeaux's equivalent of the Père La Chaise cemetery in Paris, covering 25 hectares from the church to the boulevards. Like its Parisian model, the variety of the monuments, the profusion of often touching epitaphs and its peace and quiet made it an especially romantic place in the first half of the century. Because of the number of sculptors whose works appear there, it is almost a museum of Bordeaux's 19th century stonework. It was opened in the interests of public health in 1791 and its rules were laid down by the Prefect, Charles Delacroix, the father of the famous painter. The tombs, pyramids, cippi (monumental pillars), obelisks and steles, which around 1850 were hung with a medallion bearing the portrait of the deceased, are decorated with acroteria, vases, urns, pediments, broken fluted columns, and so on, and from 1880 onwards with wreaths of everlasting flowers, crosses and angels in cast iron, and also some glass bead work. One of the original features of the cemetery is the six hundred or so chapels built between 1840 and 1930 by the great families of the city, who used the services not only of entrepreneurs and sculptors but also of the master glassmakers of Bordeaux (Villiet, Feur, Dagrant, et al.) As they could no longer be buried in the churches, they had a chapel built over their graves.

A rare representation of Death carrying his scythe on the tomb of Catherineau, a ship's captain, with the epitaph : "Thanks to science and a spirit for adventure, a seaman can brave the oceans storms for a long while, but there is a rock that he can't avoid : Death!".

Heading back to the centre, visit the new **Mériadeck district** where you will see:

- the Mussolini-style Regional Council Building (Hôtel de Région),
- the City Library (Bibliothèque Municipale), which has the most modern lending and consultation management system in France,
- the four hectares of overhead walkways,
- the complex of concrete-and-glass apartment buildings, hotels and offices, characteristic of late 20th century architecture,
- the Caisse d'Epargne savings bank, unarguably the most original work, which brings us back to the Cours d'Albret and classic Bordeaux architecture.

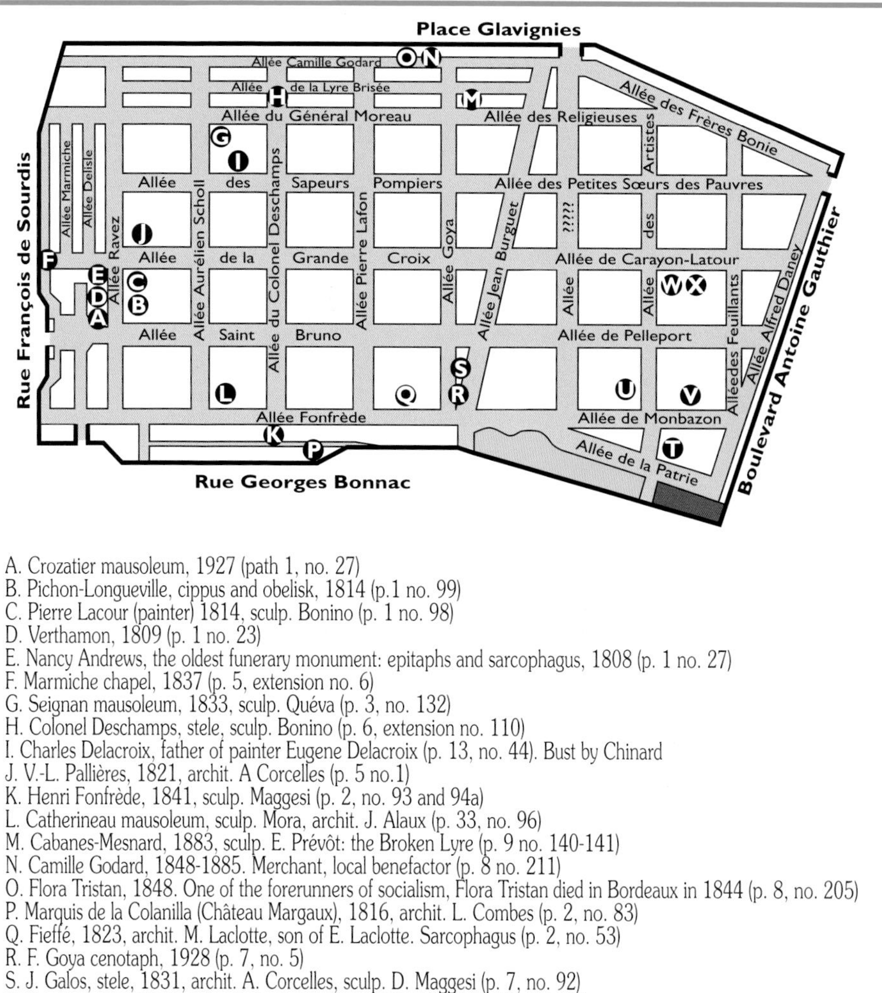

A. Crozatier mausoleum, 1927 (path 1, no. 27)
B. Pichon-Longueville, cippus and obelisk, 1814 (p.1 no. 99)
C. Pierre Lacour (painter) 1814, sculp. Bonino (p. 1 no. 98)
D. Verthamon, 1809 (p. 1 no. 23)
E. Nancy Andrews, the oldest funerary monument: epitaphs and sarcophagus, 1808 (p. 1 no. 27)
F. Marmiche chapel, 1837 (p. 5, extension no. 6)
G. Seignan mausoleum, 1833, sculp. Quéva (p. 3, no. 132)
H. Colonel Deschamps, stele, sculp. Bonino (p. 6, extension no. 110)
I. Charles Delacroix, father of painter Eugene Delacroix (p. 13, no. 44). Bust by Chinard
J. V.-L. Pallières, 1821, archit. A Corcelles (p. 5 no.1)
K. Henri Fonfrède, 1841, sculp. Maggesi (p. 2, no. 93 and 94a)
L. Catherineau mausoleum, sculp. Mora, archit. J. Alaux (p. 33, no. 96)
M. Cabanes-Mesnard, 1883, sculp. E. Prévôt: the Broken Lyre (p. 9 no. 140-141)
N. Camille Godard, 1848-1885. Merchant, local benefactor (p. 8 no. 211)
O. Flora Tristan, 1848. One of the forerunners of socialism, Flora Tristan died in Bordeaux in 1844 (p. 8, no. 205)
P. Marquis de la Colanilla (Château Margaux), 1816, archit. L. Combes (p. 2, no. 83)
Q. Fieffé, 1823, archit. M. Laclotte, son of E. Laclotte. Sarcophagus (p. 2, no. 53)
R. F. Goya cenotaph, 1928 (p. 7, no. 5)
S. J. Galos, stele, 1831, archit. A. Corcelles, sculp. D. Maggesi (p. 7, no. 92)
T. Bassié chapel, 1857, sculp. A Jouandot: Eternal Rest (1887) (p.21, no. 19)
U. Fiola vault with Egyptian female sphinxes, 1898 (p. 43, no. 10)
V. Zoé Laborde, 1912, Young Girl by G. Leroux (p. 44, no. 93a)
W. Carayon-Latour chapel, 1858 (p. 16, no. 81)
X. Fleury and Renouil de Malescas mausoleum, 1841, round temple "dedicated to death" (p. 16, no. 91-93)

(D'après P. Prévost et M. Lasserre.)

The Mériadeck district opens out from this monumental series of curved and rectangular planes, enhanced by a plate creating a stone effect.

St Michel's Tower and the Grosse Cloche from the Pey-Berland Tower.

At the corner of rue Sainte-Catherine, overlooking the terrace of Victor Louis's Grand Theatre, stands an imposing townhouse built by Laclotte, who was jealous of the theatre and said, in Gascon, "Boli l'escrabat" - "I want to knock it down". The house was commissioned by François Bonnaffé, a very rich merchant, known as "Lucky", since his merchant fleet had outsmarted the British during the American War of Independence.

The entrance to the "Galeries Bordelaises"(1831) , charming antique romantic decor.

Laubardemont house. It was from one of the windows of this house finished in 1612, that, according to certain writers, Marie de Médicis watched the Royal cortege pass during the wedding of her son Louis XIII, aged only 14, with Anne of Austria.

The crowds and the incessantly multiplying shop signs, along the two kilometres of the oldest road in Bordeaux, hide the 19th century architecture resulting from the realignment. Visitors may testify to the peculiar whim of the Bordelais who, on rainy days, invade rue Sainte-Catherine (in this case the patron saint of seamen) like snails into a ditch!

Close to the Galeries Bordelaises in rue du Pont-de-la-Mousque, the finely sculpted back entrance of the Hôtel Laubardemont, is decorated with a lion's head, with fruit and vegetables coming out of its mouth. The main front, opposite the Grand Theatre is on sober, classical lines with small heads sculpted in the corners of the windows. The Duc de Guise is supposed to have stayed there for the wedding of Louis XIII in Bordeaux in 1616.
At n. 22, **Cours du Chapeau-Rouge** (taking its name from the former hostelry whose sign bore a cardinal's hat and where, from 1464 until it was demolished in 1676, the most famous travellers stayed), Joseph Vernet, commissioned by the King to paint the ports of France, lived from 1757 to 1759.

A reduction (1773) of this statue of Louis XV on horseback by J. B. Lamoyne (1714) which was melted down during the Revolution. The king, clothed in Roman syle has great presence.

PLACE DE

The idea of a Place Royale to the glory of the sovereign dated back to 1700, but owing to opposition from the city fathers, it only materialized with the arrival of the Intendant Boucher and the plans of Jacques Gabriel, for the first time opening up the city which was still huddled behind its medieval ramparts.

It is laid out facing the river as a "half Place Vendôme" on the purest classical lines. It was built between 1729 and 1755, first by Gabriel and then his son Jacques-Ange, but was only completed in the 19th and 20th centuries when extensions were added and the Place Gabriel was created.

Façade of the Fermes house : Mercury trading with the town of Bordeaux ; sitting on bales, holds a helm stamped with the three crescents of the town. Vessels and barrels recall the water and wine, closely linked with the history of the city.

There are eight decorative pediments:

(A) Mercury trading with the city, around 1733-1740
(B) Minerva, protectress of the Arts
(C) Generosity scattering money (Francin)
(D) The Grandeur of Princes (Louis XV was to have his profile included) Francin
(E) Neptune opening the way to trade
(F) The meeting point of the Garonne and the Dordogne (Francin, 18th c.)
(G) The meeting point of the Ocean and the Mediterranean (19th c.)
(H) The Chamber of Commerce as Justice protecting the Arts, Industry, Agriculture and Navigation (19th c.)

The ground floor has arcatures and rusticated corners, a 'bel étage' (finest floor) and an attic with repeated colossal pilasters, the whole crowned by a balustrade punctuated with sculpted pediments and garrets. The buildings stand imposingly along the embankment with their high slate roofs surmounted by pinnacle turrets.

The extensive façade of the Bourse facing the Garonne.

LA BOURSE

Balcony and mascaron of the Bourse house. A timeless female face emerging from the scroll, a pattern repeated hundreds of times on façades in Bordeaux. The Louis XV style balcony is adorned with a finely carved and gilded decor.

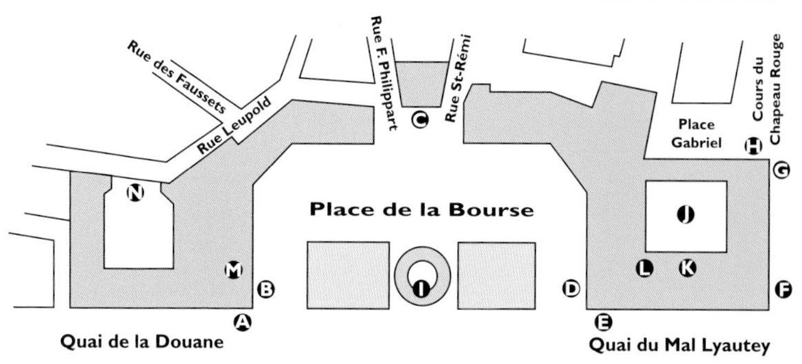

The façades are decorated with the first mascarons which were to be part of the repertoire of 18th century style with their rococo "fantaisie".
Originally, a statue of Louis XV on horseback stood in the centre of the square, but it was destroyed during the Revolution. There is a small-scale copy of it in the Musée des Arts Décoratifs and two remarkable bas-reliefs and the trophies are now in the Musée d'Aquitaine.
The Three Graces fountain (I) took the statue's place in 1869: in the centre of a stone basin on a small hexagonal pedestal stand three putti supporting a smaller cast iron basin from the top of which, their backs against a column, spring the Three Graces (traditionally Queen Victoria, Eugénie de Montijo - the future Empress - and the Queen of Spain) with hands clasped holding the amphorae.
The great hall (J), which was the last working provincial stock exchange, is built on the former courtyard of the Hôtel de la Bourse. The wrought iron rail of the main staircase (K) is by Faget (19th century) and the grille of the banister is by Dumaine (1773).
The Customs Museum (Musée des Douanes) (M) has used the volume and vaulted ceilings of the former Hôtel des Fermes to their best advantage. The inner courtyard has an 18th century fountain (N).

The Grand Pavillion and the fountain of the three Graces.

The 'Salon doré (Gilded room) in beautiful Louis XV panelling enhances the tapestry portraits of the Goblins, of the Dauphin and Marie-Antoinette on medallions and on the opposite wall of Louis XV and Marie Leczinska ; these four medallions were gifts from Nicolas Beaujon.

Further on starts the famous "Bordeaux frontage", which the Intendant Tourny wanted in order to give the city a homogeneous appearance, and sited on his orders in front of the ramparts which the Jurats (city councillors) wanted to keep. The houses are therefore like stage scenery, and very narrow in places (Quai Bourgeois). All have the same elevation, designed to make a favourable impression on visitors.
Rue Fernand-Philippart, first called rue Royale then rue de la Liberté, is lined with 18th century houses. At n. 16, the remarkable wrought iron balcony follows the curve of the building, with the windows, balcony and the brickwork forming a powerful, yet elegant ship's stem on the street corner.
Place du Parlement is the former Place du Marché Royal, which Tourny wanted to be the link between the city and its river, between the port and business. The north and south façades are the oldest, the southern one is slightly higher and breaks the harmony and alignment of the storeys; the building on the corner of rue du Parlement St. Pierre was built in the classical tradition, but in 1992!

Place du Parlement. Here is the evidence of the 'continuity of development programmes' worked towards by the spirit of Bordelais architecture for more than two centuries, mixing identical construction and reconstruction from 1760 to the present. A neo-roccoco fountain from 1865 stands in the centre.

La Maison des Aigles (Eagle's House), rue des Faussets. The narrowness of the road highlights the imposing, projecting cornices supported by sculpted corbels (busts, eagles, bucranes).

'Le Père Eternel' emerging from a cloud ; a sculpture where movement is everything, from the face to the draping of the pleating blown up by the wind, typical of Baroque art.

Rue Fernand-Philippart. A remarkable example of the ingenuity of 18th century Bordelais architects playing with finesse on the theme of rounded angles.

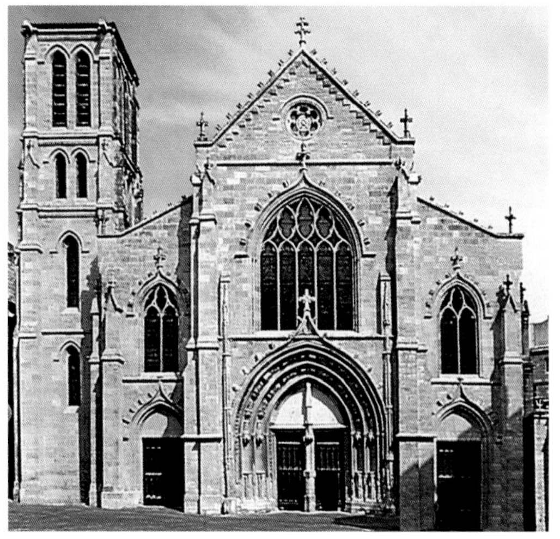

West façade of St Pierre's church renovated in the 19th century ; on the three arch mouldings of the 15th century door are successively : angels, 12 statues of the prophets carrying phylacteres and finallys foliage.

The sidestreets off rue du Parlement St. Pierre are not lacking in charm; there are 16th and 17th century houses in rue Mérignac, with obtuse angled roofs (called "Bordeaux-style"); at 12, rue des Faussets, there is a skylight with a cupola on the ground floor, where the Renaissance du Vieux Bordeaux group is working to achieve the intelligent rehabilitation of the district, and at n. 9, there is a house bearing the Imperial eagles, dating from 1810. The house has a great cornice and projecting window lintels with heavy decoration of bucranes and eagles, recalling Napoleon's Empire.
Place St. Pierre was built on the former Gallo-Roman harbour which started to silt up in the 6th century. A statue of Hercules (late 2nd or 3rd century) was found there, one of the most beautiful Gallo-Roman bronzes in France.
The 12th century church, completely rebuilt in the 14th and 15th centuries (when the sculptures over the door were done) was restored in the 19th century.
Notice the volume of the flamboyant Gothic apse. Inside, there is a remarkable 17th century Pietà and some gilded woodwork from the former reredos: statues of St. Peter and St. Paul and an "Eternal Father" giving a blessing with one hand, holding a globe in the other.
St. Pierre was the parish where the members of parliament, craftsmen, merchants and traders lived, as can be seen in the street names: rue des Bahutiers (chestmakers), rue du Cancéra (coopers), named for an old aqueduct, the "Cancer". On the corner, a niche dating from 1687 contains a recent statue of St. Peter; this was where Flora Tristan (1803-1844) died, one of the earliest feminist figures and grandmother of Gauguin.
Close by, an entry between rue Tour-de-Gassies and rue de la Cour-des-Aides leads to a courtyard where there are still ballast stone walls and renovated staircases.
Taking rue des Argentiers (goldsmiths and silversmiths who, in the 16th century, mostly made processional crosses), we come out in Place du Palais-de-l'Ombrière, where Bordeaux's parliament building once stood.

From there, we can see the **Porte Cailhau** (perhaps from "caillou", a sort of menhir, or a reminder of the ballast stones, or even the old Caillau family). This defensive gate was also built as a prestige gate, dedicated to King Charles VIII after his victory at Fornovo di Taro in 1495. As it was the traditional point of entry for the King and other great personages, it was the only one retained by Tourny in his town planning policy.

Inside the gate, the first floor, from where the gap into which the portcullis was drawn up can be seen under the floor, was where the troops were housed. The Tourist Office runs an exhibition on the history of the gate and Old Bordeaux. (In season: 10 am to 1 pm and 2 pm to 6 pm; out of season: Saturdays, 2 pm to 6 pm). The second floor (mullioned windows) was originally only accessible from the ramparts. On the top floor, used for defensive purposes, the machicolations (a small, crenellated gallery with wooden shutters) hides the narrow wall walk.

In front, nearer the river, Tourny's "façade" of harmonious houses continues. The rusticated arches on the ground floor have a half-storey, typical of 18th century Bordeaux. They are decorated with mascarons, every one of which is different; their verve and rococo "fantaisie" extends all along the embankments.

Quai Richelieu: three sailors with hats at n. 4, feminine figures at n. 7, a mulatto at n. 14, a satyr (perhaps) at n. 18, a Turk at n. 32, and at n. 38 there is Bacchus, just as much at home here as Mercury and Neptune in this city of wine, trade and seafaring. This has been called the "Caribbean Façade" of Bordeaux, stretching along the embankments, for it could not have been built without the prosperity from its trade with the islands, nor could the Place Royale have been completed.

The river God, or Neptune as a child, at the helm above two keystones, is proof of the high quality of façade decor during the 18th century.

Porte Cailhau was the recognised entrance for royals and other important people making official visits to the town : François I in 1526, Eléonore of Portugal, sister of Charles Quint in 1530, Marie de Médicis in 1616 etc.

Bordeaux as seen from the opposite bank. The outstanding view of the town from the Bastide takes in the whole history of the town in a single glance. From the impressive 114 m spire of St Michel to the prestigious monumental façade realised by the great Intendants, an awe-inspiring sight for the disembarking visitor.

Richelieu Quay

Porte de Bourgogne, or des Salinières.

The **Porte de Bourgogne** (or Porte des Salinières) was built by Portier and Gabriel between 1750 and 1755 to replace a medieval gate. The classical style triumphal arch, adorned with twin columns on the river side and a Doric cornice, should have been decorated with a great sculptured motif, which was never commenced.

The play of light along a road in old Bordeaux.

Rue de la Rousselle is lined with 18th and 19th century houses. This was where the salted fish merchants were centred. They were said to be hard-working and rich (Montaigne's grandfather made his fortune that way), but their activities caused a sickening stench throughout the district.
The adjacent streets are not lacking in charm: rue du Soleil (from Soler, one of the great Bordeaux families of the Middle Ages) with its run-down houses; Place Raymond Colon (another Bordeaux family, rivals of the Solers) has a typical 16th-17th century house with its staircase visible under the arches where a sundial and trompe-l'oeil adorn the wall since it was restored. Rue Descazeaux, which has kept the same name since 1400, has preserved the carriage gateways of its former houses.
Head back up rue de la Rousselle where we find once more alternating gates and shops, have a look at n. 33 on the corner of the narrow rue du Muguet - "Lily of the Valley Street", a reminder of the gardens that once bordered it; at n. 23-25, where Montaigne was married in 1565 (he lived there until 1570) the vestiges of the family's private chapel can still be seen buried under later building work.

Impasse de la rue Neuve : the house of Jeanne de Lartige, the wife of Montesquieu. Controlled elegance and decor in one of the rare 16th century houses in Bordeaux, with its typical gallery.

Impasse de la rue Neuve. The two gothic windows with identical arcatures rest on the small columns surmounted on a radiating quatrefoil. They have been preserved despite the obvious other changes made to the building.

At 15, rue Neuve, a street full of doctors at one time, a corner niche contains a statue of the Virgin Mary; at the bottom of the cul-de-sac, some lovely windows are the only vestiges of Gothic civil architecture. In the courtyard, beyond the vaulted porch, is the house of Montesquieu's wife, Jeanne de Lartigue, typical of the 16th century: a staircase in a turret leads up to the galleries of the upper floors and apartments. On the ground floor, under the two flattened arches decorated with the busts of the husband and wife, there was a shop. In this house, Protestants first worshipped in Bordeaux, an act later to be banned by Parliament in 1531.

The nearby Place Jean Bureau (mayor of Bordeaux in 1453) is lined with 16th century houses, including the impressive house of Arnaud de Ferron (n. 21-23), a legal expert, friend of the Bordeaux humanists and of La Boétie. Montaigne used to have meetings with his friends in this district.
To the left, a series of façades along rue Renière ; to the right, on rue Teulère are some beautiful false balconies (n. 12) leading to the north wall of St Eloi's Church, which joins onto the Grosse Cloche, symbolic of Bordeaux's identity.
In rue **St James**, a road dominated for a long time by printers and bookshops, stands the now much changed house of Simon de Millanges at no. 28, who held a publishing monopoly from 1572 to 1623. From his presses came Montaignes 'Les Essays' as well as the works of local humanists. Further down, at n. 18, a small, ornately sculpted door with foliated scrolls in light relief is part of a beautiful Renaissance house. At the corner of rue P. de Coubertin coming back up rue St James, is the house in which Etienne de la Boétie lived in 1559, author of "A treatise on voluntary servitude" and a friend of Montaigne.
The Grosse Cloche is the last surviving remnant from the 13th century fortified gate of St Eloi, which provided an entrance, through the double walls of this sophisticated fortification, and protected this district of aldermen, tradespeople and craftsmen. Two towers on each wall framed two smaller turrets in the middle. The two towers on the rear wall, away from the moat, form the present Grosse Cloche, the vault and bays of which were altered in 1449 and the towers raised.
St Eloi's Church (patron saint of goldsmiths, silversmiths and gunsmiths, many of whom worked in this district : hence rue des Argentiers (silversmiths) and rue des Faures) was the location, once a year of a ceremony during which new aldermen were sworn in, in the name of Christ, a ceremony known as 'the Jurade'. This 14th century building was built on the foundations of the defensive wall (obsolete a century after its construction) with the church tower in one of its turrets. The three doors correspond to the three naves inside the church, restored by Poitevin in 1828.
At n. 51-53 **Cours Victor-Hugo**, the Impasse de la Fontaine-Bouquière (a Tourist Office visit) is the site of the last remains of the double ramparts topped with semi-circular turrets, a postern and evidence of the use of ballast stones in the construction. These stones, coming from France and the rest of Europe, used to arrive with barrels that then left full of 'claret' as the English like to call Bordeaux wine. Opposite the Grosse Cloche, the Montaigne College has replaced the Jesuit School. Despite 19th century alterations, the 17th century architecture is still recognisable. On the corner of Cours Victor-Hugo and Cours Pasteur, the Aquitaine Museum, specialising in the history of the region, has been set up in what was the home of the Faculty of Sciences and Arts, where the Cenotaph of Montaigne may be seen.
On rue des Ayres, alongside St Paul's Church, stands the "Mairerie", the former residence of the town's mayor, which has retained its original square medieval tower and gothic style windows, but is difficult to get to today. It is the last remaining example of an "oustau" (fortified) house from the Middle Ages once very common in Bordeaux.

The Grosse Cloche. The bell of the old belfry from the Middle Ages joined to the aldermens house rang for all the great public events up to the Liberation. As punishment for the revolt of the Bordelais, Henry II had the bell and clock taken down in 1548. The fire in the Town Hall in 1657 required major restoration work which continued up to the Revolution and included the fitting of ironwork and a new clock.

The Tower of the Mairerie : official residence of the mayor in the Middle Ages up to 1620, Montaigne must have lived there.

The steps of the Impasse de la Fontaine-Bouquière lead from the road separating the two walls of the rampart built in the 13th century. It was then at the ground level of the town.

The "Mairerie", which has since become a presbytry is decorated with an arched gallery incorporating projecting archstones, typical decoration of the period (1618) now hidden by the surrounding buildings.
St Paul's Church, which used to be the Jesuits Professed House, is typical of the development of the baroque style in Bordeaux : the façade and ground plan being inspired by the church of Gésu in Rome. It was built from 1663 to 1676 with the bell-tower following in the 19th century. Inside, above the main altar, stands the impressive group sculpture in marble of the Deification of St François-Xavier, a masterpiece that Guillaume Coustou installed in 1748.

The Exaltation of St François-Xavier : the saint, on a cloud, with an expressive gesture, receives the martyr's palm from a cherub ; the ensemble is put in relief by the gold background and polychromed marble of the altar piece.

The raised gallery from 1618 to 1619 illustrates the ternary rythym (three levels, three bays) often employed during the Renaissance. It allowed movement between the various main parts of the building.

Place Fernand-Lafargue was in an enclosed area, and the site of the Bordeaux market, an important centre of the town's activity. It included butchers and fishmongers stalls and the 'clie' where fish were fileted. The pillory was also to be found here. Opinions are formed through conversations. In 1633, the Duke d'Epernon who was opposed to Archbishop Henri de Sourdis, due to his rights over the 'clie', forbade the servants of the prelate to go there. A few days later he came to blows with the archbishop. The affair blew up and the whole population of the town, clergy included, were divided over it.

There were scuffles in the street and the Capucin friars came down on the side of the Duke! The following year, the Duke apologised honorably at Coutras, bringing the affair to a conclusion.
Rue Pas-Saint-Georges takes you to the crossroads with rue du Loup and du Cerf-Volant. At the far end of the latter, at n. 47-49 rue des Bahutiers, are two beautiful 15th to 17th century houses with their original gables ; this is no longer the case in rue du Loup, at the corner with rue A. Miqueu, where an unfortunate conversion of the top floor has completely changed the character of one of the very few half-timbered houses left in Bordeaux. This section of **rue du Loup** was inhabited by painters in the Middle Ages before being taken over by cutlers in the 18th century.

Rue des Bahutiers. A narrow gable giving onto the road (steeply sloping roofs in the "French style") and opening out to the rear are typical of the arrangement of Bordeaux houses in the Middle Ages with the shops stall under the ample arcade of the ground floor (15th and 16th centuries). Next to it, the 16th to 17th century house has an obtuse angle roof in the "Bordeaux style".

A stone and half-timbered house. The top floor has been remodelled. A drawing by Fontan from around 1900 shows it with a gable in the "Bordeaux style" (rue du Loup).

Rue Sainte-Catherine has been the "High Street" and main shopping area since the days of ancient Burdigala. Half-way along is Place St-Projet, where an 18th century fountain, backed onto a building, used to supply water to the whole district. St Projet's Church, of which only the remains of the bell-tower are still visible, was the meeting place for a number of trade guilds (tapestry makers, glassmakers, the brotherhood of St Roch and St Sebastian), and during Lent, well known preachers came to speak.
Rue Guérin, which leads off from rue de Loup, was the site of the first incidents which sparked off the so-called "stamped paper" revolt in 1675 against the taxation system imposed by Louis XIV.
The Ragueneau house at n. 71 has an austere, tied wall front, not in keeping with the decoration (mid-17th century) which evokes the range of mannerist sculpture (panels of fantasy lions). The main door and its undulating vault date from

Fountain, Place St-Projet. The front of the base is decorated with an old crossroad type cross.

the first quarter of the 18th century.
Since Gallo-Roman times, the quarters of St Christoly and Puy-Paulin have been the focus of the town's activity. Everything from before the 17th century (other then the cellars which are reminders of the "Roman castrum" and the river Devèze flowing unobserved) has been replaced by 18th and 19th century developments and even more radically by 20th century constructions. At the end of rue du Père Louis de Jabrun, the Morel house has a beautiful entrance dating from 1730, crowned with a wrought iron balustrade. The austere interior elevations contrast with the magnificence of the vaulted passageway in which a

door is hung with two intricately sculpted leaves. Rue Poquelin-Molière is named in memory of the visit in 1656 of the actor who performed in what was the real tennis court, located at the corner of rue du Temple.
On rue de Grassi, it is worth noting the Perrier de Larsan house (circa 1750) credited to the architect Portier. In place Jean Moulin, the site of the Jean Moulin National Centre, Resistance Museum, stands Antonin Mercié's "Gloria Victis", one of the most famous plastic art illustrations of the 'Revanche' (Revenge) movement which followed the Franco-Prussian War in 1870, highlighting heroism, in spite of the defeat, of the soldiers who died for their country.

A ringed knocker in the shape of a toad's thigh from the time of Louis XVI.

The Morel house (9, rue Poquelin Molière) is adorned with a beautiful Louis XVI style door.

Gloria Victis.
A. Mercié initially designed his 'Fame' in 1870 with outstretched wings to carry in his arms a victorious soldier which he then had to replace by this young and handsome victim, a moving hero of this sad defeat.

Of the church dating from the end of the 11th century, in which Urbain II preached in 1096, only the west wall (1) and the N-W/S-E orientation for the transept remain. It was in the first, large church that Eleanor of Aquitaine was married in 1137. With her financial support, the construction of the nave (possibly with a cupola) was undertaken. In the 13th century, the bays were opened up and modified and the walls raised. The vaults were rebuilt in the two centuries that followed, and reinforced with buttresses.
The Royal Door (2) was situated in 1250 between the archbishops walls. Breaking with tradition, the chancel and transept were erected from east to west in the 13th and 14th centuries, the radiating section of the apse being based on Amiens Cathedral, after 1270, with its double ring of side aisles, the outside one made into side-chapels.
The chancel was built with the help of funds allocated by Archbishop Bertrand de Goth (1264 to 1314) who was informed here, on the 20th of June 1305, that he had just been elected as Pope. Clement V became the first Pope from Avignon and confirmed the primatiat of the cathedral. Around 1400 the major work on the south façade and the rose window was finished ; the upper sections of the tower and the north façade were built in the 16th century. 175 years passed, from Pope Clement V to King François I before the construstion was complete. In this time, the Black Prince had assembled all the nobility to pay hommage to him in 1363; Pey Berland, who founded the University of Bordeaux in 1444, was the last archbishop under the English Guyenne. On the 25th of November 1615, Louis XIII married Anne of Austria in St André's, passing, according to legend, through the Royal Door, that no-one should ever use again. A fodder store during the Revolution, Combes restored the nave and raised the floor level by 1.80 m in 1804. Abadie, the architect who designed Sacré-Coeur in Montmartre, built the sacristy in 1878 on the site of the 12th century cloisters that had just been demolished. Over the last 30 years, the cathedral, which has hosted numerous concerts, is constantly being restored.

The tympanum of the Royal Door

The radiating apse, the elevation of the chancel and the two spires over the North Door of the cathedral seen from the terrace of the Pey-Berland Tower. The church is listed as world heritage as part of the Saint Jacques de Compostelle pilgrim paths.

In spite of the mixed styles of its construction, entering by the West Door gives you a striking view of the width of the nave (16 m), the height of the plain chancel, and the slight offset, after rebuilding, of the transept crossing. The 16th century organ loft is surmounted by a more recent organ chest. Below, two Renaissance bas-reliefs, taken from the old jube : the Resurrection (A) and the Descent to the Underworld (B) (Pluto and Persephony in the latter, an eagle in the former seem more closely related to the world of mythology than to the Bible).

The pulpit sculpted by Cabirol has come from the church of St Rémi.

Near the transept is the tomb of Cardinal de Cheverus who died in 1836 (C).

In 1889, at the transept crossing (D), Archbishop Guilbert was buried in the recess, surmounted by radiating gables, originally of Canon Raymond de Landiras who died in 1362. Nearby is a holy-water basin bearing the arms of Sourdis.

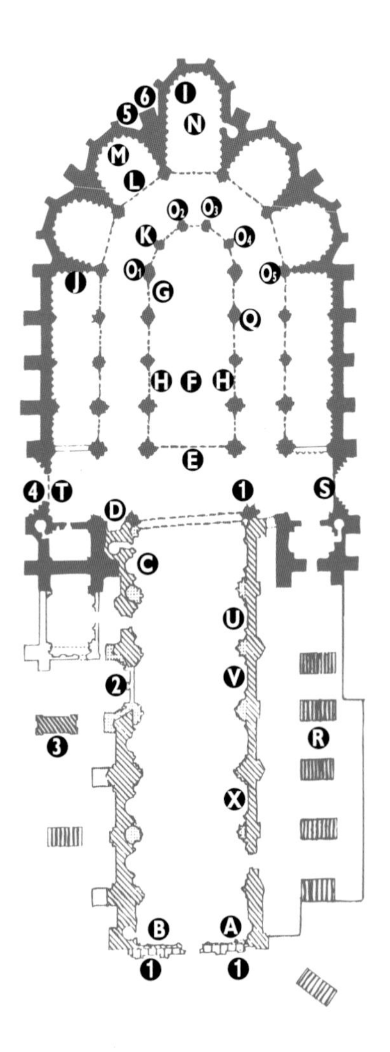

An alabaster statue of St Martial holding out the Epistle to the people of Bordeaux, an apocryphal book in one hand and the staff given to him by St Peter in the other. The emaciated forms and the styling of the face accentuate the spirituality which radiates from this image of the legendary founder of the Church in Bordeaux. It is the finest example of an alabaster sculpture (15th century) under the English Guyenne.

A superb collection of wrought ironwork (E) screen the chancel, doors, grills and credences, made by Charlut (18th century). On the floor a mosaic from Hippone, sent by Monsignor Dupuch, the first Algerian archbishop after the conquest of Algeria (F). The stalls come from St Bruno's church (G). The two episcopal thrones made by the neo-classical Bordelais sculpters Quéva and Bonino date from when worship restarted in the cathedral under Napoleon (H).

The organ loft above the entrance of the west front.

In this delicately carved bas-relief of the "Descent into the Underworld" which decorates the very old jube there is a hint of a pagan influence (Pluto and Persephone?).

The side and radiating apsidal chapels are all faced with genuine neo-gothic decor and fittings provided by Monsignor Donnet from 1850. The finest Bordelais glassmaker of the time, Joseph Villiet, was made responsible for the glassware in 1852. In the axial chapels, the Good Shepherd and the Madonna and Child (I).
Mont Carmel's Chapel (J) is dedicated to St Simon Stock, a Carmelite friar who died in Bordeaux in 1265, and who is buried under the altar. Above the altar, the albaster wall statue in the nave of Our Lady is reminiscent, in style and material, of the English alabaster work of the 14th century. Opposite, in the ambulatory, an alabaster wall statue of St Martial (K) of a quite different quality, seeming to draw from its almost translucid material the austere and ascetic atmosphere which surrounds it. It is not a typical example of this type of work, unlike the two bas-reliefs of the Assumption and the Resurrection in the chapel opposite (L). In this, St Margaret's Chapel, is a restored statue of St Martha (M) who used to be, as would be expected, the doorway to the old 16th century St André's hospital. In the axial chapel (N), the 16th century corner spandrels recount the story of the infancy of Christ, with tremendous attention to detail in the depiction of the characters ; the Annunciation, Visitation, Nativity, Circumcision, Massacre of the Innocents and the Escape to Egypt. In the ambulatory, are a succession of more recent works : the tomb of Cardinal Andrieu de Malric (O1), a "Mater amablis" (02) by D. Magessi (1860) and Our Lady of Mont Carmel (03) situated next to the tomb of Cardinal Lecot (04) and Joan of Arc by Bourdelle from the start of the 20th century (05).

St Anne and the Blessed Virgin.

A certain sobriety is created by the chancel built by B. Dechamps (circa 1320) with impressive clusters of arcades made up of small columns rising above the stalls, surmounted by the triforium, above which are the top windows.

On the corner is the anonymous masterpiece of a sculptor from the end of the Middle Ages in Bordeaux, of St Anne and the Blessed Virgin (Q). This very young mother was possibly one of a group of "Three Marys" (the three sisters) venerated by the people of Bordeaux. The harmonious attitudes of the group and the natural quality and softness in the faces is an example of the "detente" (relaxed) mood which influenced sculpture around 1500.
In the sacristies built by Abadie, the decor and stained-glass window depict the archbishops of Bordeaux (R).
In the transept, the two rose windows "to the Blessed Virgin" facing south (S) and to "Christ on the Cross and St André" to the north (T) have been well restored. On the south side, the nave is adorned with three beautiful, classical 17th century paintings ; the Resurrection of Christ by A. Tuchi (U), a moving Christ on the Cross from 1635 by Jacob Jordaens, a pupil of Rubens (V), and "Christ before Caiphas" possibly the work of Hontorst (X).

The exterior

The north and south sides are delicately decorated with flying buttressess and pinnacles, crockets and cabbage leaves. The numerous alterations to the nave required the addition of 8 buttresses in the 15th and 16th century. The most recent, supporting the Royal Door in the Renaissance style, bears the date 1533, and the arms of Cardinal-Archbishop Charles de Gramont (3).

The lower level of the Royal Door (2) shows the floor level of the cathedral in the 13th century. It's theme, the Last Judgement, should normally be on the West Door, as is the case in other large cathedrals, but at the time, it was the only place where it could be located to face the Bishop's Palace and the city. The work carried out in the 19th century disturbed the order and condition of the Apostles.
On the tympanum, the first register shows the resurrection of all classes of society : the crowns of Kings, mitres of Bishops, a woman's 'touret' (a fashionable hairstyle under St Louis) and a Jew's cap. The second register shows the supplication of Christ by the Blessed Virgin and St John, kneeling, surrounded by angels carrying trumpets and instruments from the Passion. On the top register angels carrying the Sun and Moon to the centre. Four arch mouldings successively display 10 adoring angels, 10 more celebrating the Eucharist, 4 seraphims and 6 women martyrs, with finally the "sages" of the Old Testament. On the upper gallery, some of the 10 bishops and kings have been recently renovated. The 10 apostles on the piedroits are supported on modern pedestals. Under the platform which covers their heads are the capitals of the columns that they are mounted against. On the left a beardless St John, St Jacques-le-Mineur or St Philippe with the stone of the martyr and St Bartholemew with a knife. On the right, possibly St Paul, bald and bearded. The classical styling, the serenity on the faces, the exaggerated pleating and the natural feel of the foliage is a reminder of the great doors of the Ile-de-France such as Notre-Dame or St Chapelle.
The North Door (4) used to support the spires, and faced the largest square in the city. With its picturesque, undercut decor and its iconography, it links itself with the Spanish tympanums of the 14th century (Pamplona). The triumphant Church (the Last Supper, Ascension and the Last Judgement) reply to the militant Church on the piedroits (although it iis difficult to clearly identify the Popes and prelates). The statue on the pier, possibly symbolically, may be St Peter.
The arboresence of the apse may be appreciated from the top of the Pey-Berland tower it contains empty niches with only two elegant 14th century statues escaping revolutionary fervour : Mary Magdelene with her weight on one foot, in rich, middle class clothes bearing her pot of ointment (5) and St André (6) without a piece of the cross (it was in the 14th century that the cross was attributed to him in the form of an X).

The **Pey-Berland Tower**, named after the Girondin archbishop, was originally separated from the cathedral by the canon houses, according to a custom popular throughout all western France for isolating the spire. Documents confirm that it was indeed a bell-tower, designed to complement the impact of the church. It is a square based tower, supported by solid buttresses up to the two levelled open floor where the bells are situated. From a terrace, supported on a level of false bays, rises an octagonal tower, the top of which, rebuilt after 1850, has been crowned with "Our Lady of Aquitaine", 6.5 m tall in spun, gilded copper (Visiting hours from 10 am to 12:30 pm and 2 pm to 6 pm, 360 days a year).

The Pey-Berland Tower looking over the impressive St André's Cathedral.

The South Door (1250-1330) damaged during the Revolution, was consecrated to the Blessed Virgin as indicated by the three arch mouldings, through which can be seen passing wise virgins, then mad virgins and then apostles. The niches are empty and the stylobates are enclosed with quatrefoils. The story is recounted of St Martial who was the (legendary) founder of the cathedral, and was named as the first bishop.
Squeezed in between the canon houses, this door looked towards the ramparts and the du Peuge river, the only remaining indication of which is the stepped line of the houses on rue des Palanques, opposite the door. The road marks the route of the stream, now sub-terranean, that used to be crossed on moveable planks ("palanques" in the Bordelais dialect) up to the 19th century.
This road leads to the façade of the Chapelle des Filles de Notre Dame, which became a chapel of the Reformed Church in 1805. This congregation, founded by the niece of Montaigne, Jeanne de Lestonnac, was devoted to educating young girls, but was far from being the most successful of its time. For this reason, young people from the Reformed movement were taken from their families and placed there by order. The chapel, built from 1625 to 1626 has a remarkable ternary rythym elevation : three niches and three openings (doors and oculi). The legibility of form, their overlapping and the exaggerated scrolls result in a most harmonious monument.

Not far from here are the remains of the Fort du Hâ, built from around 1454 to 1470 to the end of the Hundred Years' War. Its vast area (120 m by 68 m) provided space for a large keep flanked by buttresses and watch towers at the corners, and with the whole fort covered with a high slate roof. The brother of Louis XI, the Duke of Aquitaine, Charles de Valois lived and died there ; in the 17th century it became the official residence of the Governor and Lieutenant Generals of Guyenne. Of the original construction, only two towers remain, the gunpowder tower and the horseshoe shaped west tower, known as the English tower, possibly from the time of the English occupation. It was also used as a prison during the Revolution. It held non-juring priests, and more curiously 235 captured English and Portugese sailors and 27 American Indians who were with them in 1798. It was demolished in 1835.

The impressive block of the Round Tower or Gunpowder Tower of Fort du Hâ, built under Charles VII.

Harmonious in its deceptive simplicity, the façade of the Chapel on rue du Hâ, illustrates, with its overlapping and carefully positioned forms, the aesthetics so important to the Baroque style in the 17th century.

The **Palais Rohan** (Town Hall) was built in the 18th century to replace the medieval Bishop's palace built onto the side of the cathedral which was becoming decrepit. After the initial project was abandoned in 1768, Monsignor Mériadec de Rohan sold the marshy land between the cathedral and St Bruno, which is now the 'Mériadeck district' to finance the construction of a new Bishop's palace.

The Great Door

The palais

Hebe pouring some wine for Love, who, still young, soon falls asleep under the effect of the nectar, taken in by the ruse, and so stays near to her for longer.

The entry porch (A) which seals off the courtyard has eight archway openings and frames a monumental door with columned avant-corps and alcoves decorated with 19th century statues of geniuses of the Sciences and Arts on one side and of Trade and Industry on the other. The low vaulted porch with Tuscan columns is reminiscent of the style modelled on classical antiquity intro-

The Palais Rohan and the main courtyard

duced by Victor Louis. Framed by two low wings, the main part of the building (B) is laid out on the ground floor supporting colossal, lightly projecting Ionic order pilasters scanning the whole façade, decorated by Cabirol, of the Wise Evangelic Woman destroyed during the Revolution and replaced by a clock!

The garden façade (C), extended with 2 low, lateral wings, repeat the same themes as in the courtyard but with a triangular façade adorned with a statue symbolising "liberality"

Inside, the panelled Louis XVI rooms (D) are embellished with plant patterns created by Cabirol from 1782-86.The dining room (E) has a "trompe l'œil" decor in a Pompei style, painted by Berinzago and continued by one of his students for the deceptive architecture and the ceiling. Lacour was responsible for the greying. The designs above the doors represent the seasons, the panels a sacrifice to Ceres and an offering to Pomona and the false niches support two "trompe l''oeil" statues ; Hebe on one side and Bacchus on the other, modelled on a classically antique Apollo. It is said that it was in watching Lacour restore his

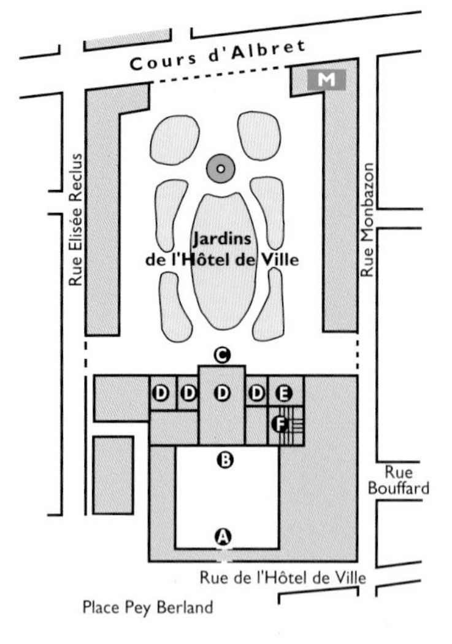

own works of Art in 1804 that Delacroix, the son of the prefect and only a child at the time, discovered his vocation.
The monumental staircase (F), is a masterpiece of stereotomy (the art of working with stones) based on deceptive angles and embellished on the landing with a radiating sun pattern. The wrought iron bannisters with the handrail on the right in the style of Louis XVI was made by Jayer. In the town council chambers, the decor, busts, furniture embossed with the Bordeaux crescents and the reserved seating (stepped rows of seating for the public, counsellors benches, the rostrum for the Mayor and his administration) are perfect examples of the prestigious role that mayor's liked to take during the Third Republic.
The much changed garden is framed with two wings built around 1880 to house the Bordeaux Museums, now the Museum of Fine Arts. Faget's iron gates are a good example of the renewal of interest for the 18th century style in Bordeaux, after 1850.

The Main Room

The garden side

The Main Staircase

Started by J. Etienne in 1772, the construction was completed by R. F. Bonfin, the town architect ; the interior fittings were finished during the episcopate of Monsignor Champion de Cicé in 1786 just before the Revolution, when it became an administrative office, housing in the right wing, redeveloped by Combes, the civil and criminal courts. In 1835, it became the Town Hall, having served as the Prefecture, Imperial and Royal Palace. Further along **Cours d'Albret**, the Poissac house is adorned with a door from the Pichon house (Cours de l'Intendance). It was one of the first houses built (1775) on the land divided up by the archbishop. Along with the Basquiat house next to it (n. 29), the façades reflect the same sober intentions of the Palais Rohan.

The Poissac house from the garden of the Town Hall

Porte Dijeaux : the front view looking from place Gambetta.

The de Lalande house (1779). Two centuries later, walk into the beautiful, paved courtyard, after noticing the door knocker, and imagine yourself going back in time to the town at the time of the Revolution, in the house that M. de Lalande had just settled into.

Going back up **rue Bouffard**, a road full of antique dealers and art galleries, the old Lalande house, built by Laclotte in the 18th century, in the classic form of a house between a courtyard and a garden (the latter has now been developed on) which has become the Museum of Decorative Arts.

The painted ceilings of the Pichon house

At the far end of this road, **Place Gambetta** has been built on one of the most unpleasant sites of the old town, where drains were used as a refuse dump and, near Saint Seurin, were filled with the uncleared rubble from houses destroyed during the insurrection of the Fronde (1648-53). Its construction started in 1747, and in 1770 it was dedicated, with the name "Place Dauphin", to Marie Antoinette on the occasion of her marriage with the future king, Louis XVI. The present uniform collection with its facade of mascarons wasn't completed until the 19th century. The oldest mascarons, around Porte Dijeaux and rue des Remparts, embellish the façades not only with their plastic baroque effect, but with the often quasi-Rabelasian liveliness of some of them; a smiling adolescent face with his bagpipes, the portrait of a street urchin laughing at his lessons, the Sun and Moon in company with the two neighbouring mascarons, Ceres'hair changing into an ear of corn etc.

Porte Dijeaux (1748) is surmounted with a façade showing the arms of France and a strange lion on the keystone facing the square. The town's symbol and a bearded head (Neptune) are sculpted on the road side.

Go down **Cours de l'Intendance**, to a beautiful 18th century house remodelled with a balustrade and flame ornaments, just before the restaurant, in what was the Pichon house (President of the Bordeaux parliament in the 17th century). The door relocated in cours d'Albret left room for three large arcades supported by atlantes of the "Once Beautiful Gardener". Inside, on the first floor, is an original ceiling supported by beams decorated with flowers in the mannerist tradition, reflecting the taste for herbs introduced at the start of the 17th century.

The landscaped garden of Place Gambetta

Great centuries and small details.

Maison Frugès : grill.
Grand Theatre : panelling.
Bas relief by Cabirol.
Console on Cours Victor Hugo.
Monument to the Girondins: cock.
Grosse Cloche : the clock.
Mascaron of Ceres.
Decor of a chemists.
Symbol of Bordeaux.
Grand Theatre : the eulogy of music.
Door knocker. 6th century sarcophagus decor.

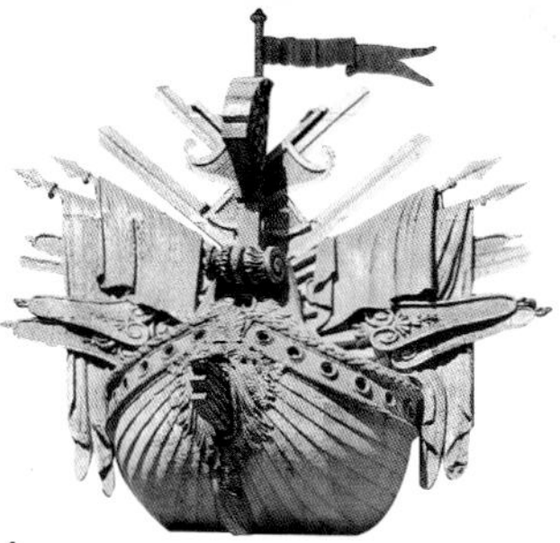

After the fire in 1755, which damaged the Town Hall, (near to the Grosse Cloche), that housed the old theatre, 18 years of discussions and debates between the Jurade, Parliament and the Intendant passed before finally the Duke of Richelieu, governor of Guyenne, was able to nominate his architect Victor Louis and start the work on the new building which was inaugurated in 1780 after many problems.
The **Grand Theatre**, his most famous work, along with the galleries of the Royal Palace and the French Theatre in Paris, provided not only a superb example of neo-classical architecture but also the prototype for future Parisian and indeed European theatres from the end of the 18th century to the start of the 20th century, with entrance halls, foyers, multi-purpose rooms (concert halls), meeting rooms, indeed a cafe and even a shop when it first opened.
In the 19th century the concert hall was unfortunately remodelled as a ballroom, then into a Grand Foyer, with the access to the hall changed. During the dark years of 1870 and 1914 the theatre became the seat of the National Assembly.
The restorations carried out in recent years have brought back the 18th century decor, tarnished since the Revolution by the oil lighting of the time.

The enormous peristyle, façade of the Grand Theatre, nicknamed "Louis' twelve columns".

Erato, muse of music, Minerva leaning on his shield, Juno with her peacock, as well as nine other statues (copies) adorn the terrace of the Grand Theatre, each one directly above one of the columns of the peristyle.

The Grand Theatre

The neo-classical façade is made up of 12 collosal columns, of the composite order, supporting a large cornice on which stand 12 statues at the front of a terrace, representing the 9 muses and 3 goddesses (Juno, Venus and Minerva) the work of Berruer and Van den Drix (A).

The decorated coffered ceiling which covers the peristyle is an example of the technical expertise of the time. The main steps were built around 1850 at the same time as the ground level around the theatre was lowered ; the galleries running the length of the side façades (B), which were then at road level and housed shops, have been completed with balustrades.

Inside, the spacious, columned entrance hall (C), supports what was the oval concert hall and provided access to the grandiose stairwell (D) nearly 20 m high in which shadow and light interplay in the best neo-palladian tradition. Striking embossed work surrounds the three-flighted stairs in an antique style decor with caryatids, a central door façade and niches adorned with statues sculpted by Dumilâtre (end of the 19th century). At the top of the stairs, the loggias of the "bel étage" (finest floor) adorned with Ionic columns and balustered balconies, lead to the foyers and to one of the levels looking over the stage. All the loggias around the stairwell (crowned with a large cupola) and the "gods" foyer are scanned with cupolas and arches.

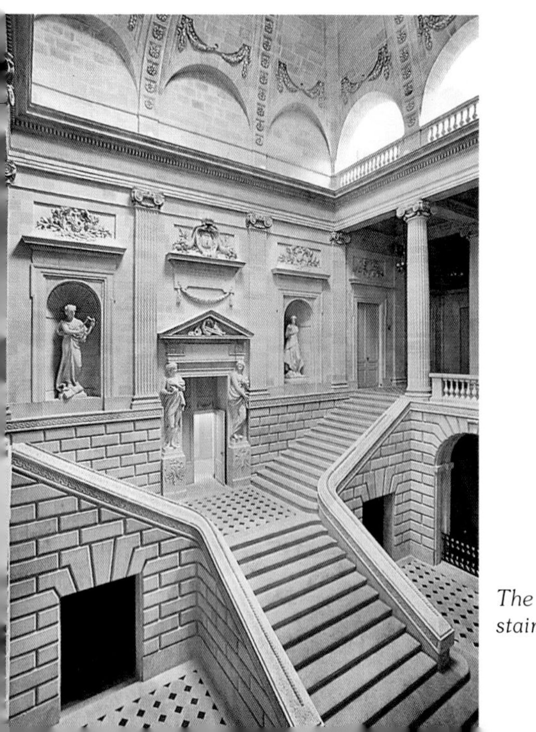

The stairwell

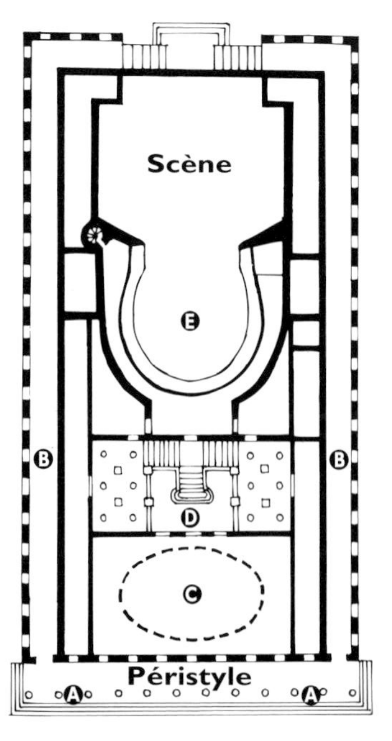

The ceiling above the stage.

The original blue and gold colours of the actual theatre area have been restored along with its scenic decor ; the painting of a long gallery of columns to deceive the eye and extend the vista of the theatre, interspersed with pillars between the boxes and the balconies.
The boxes appear to be unsupported with the projection of the balustered balconies.
The spiral arches, with a reducing effect of lunettes and half domes, converge to the circular ceiling, repainted in 1917 by Roganeau, a Bordelais artist, based on the original trompe l'œil painting of Robin. It represents the town of Bordeaux offering the theatre to Apollo and the muses.
Gildings, foliated scrolls and camaieus of elements associated with the decor as well as grotesque ornaments on the doors of the boxes have rediscovered their original freshness.

The sumptuous decor of the area around the stage

Between the Grand Theatre and the river are a block of houses known as the "îlot Louis", built from 1774 to 1778 for the upper middle class families of the time. The Saige house has all the airs of a Roman palace revised in a neo-classical style. Along the whole length of the îlot, its balustered balconies rest on consoles and no longer on pendentives. In 1789, the Café des Etrangers could be found here, a political group with ideas ahead of its time, later to become

The entrance hall of the Saige house. Louis played here on the theme of curves : flattened and surbased vaults, arcades, ellipses and impressive patterns on the ceiling.

the first revolutionary society in Bordeaux, called the Club du Café National. A certain uniformity, as was designed by Victor Louis, continues along the whole façade ; usually high, arcatures with a mezzanine, wrought iron balcony supported by consoles on the finest floor, a large number of floors, a crowning balustrade and finally, small scale sculpted decorations.
At n.1 cours Chapeau Rouge, the high door of the Boyer-Fonfrède house conceals a vaulted, panelled passageway, closed off by a wrought iron grill which controls access to the appartments (a typical Bordelais feature) ; from the entrance hall rises one of the most remarkable staircases in Bordeaux, a superb, vast spiral, seemingly unsupported, in a single, uninterrupted movement.
It is said that Hausmann, the Prefect of Bordeaux used to find the source of his inspiration looking at the elevation of these façades. At the far corner, the La Molère or de Fumel house, (also with rounded angles), from where the Schopenhauers used to observe the wine market that they so vividly described, contains some elements of the decoration and furniture of the period. Impressive door knockers still adorn several of the houses, particularly along rue Esprit des Lois (in honour of Montesquieu, the first President of the Bordeaux parliament), which leads back to the Place de la Comèdie. Here, the 16 bays of the impressive façade of the Rolly house (started by Victor Louis, modified and completed in the 19th century) give way to the peristyle of the Grand Theatre.

Boyer-Fonfrède house. Constructed by Victor Louis, the remarkable stairway soon became famous : a man on horseback once rode up to the 3rd floor, and a friend wrote to the owner at the address "To Mr Fonfrède, on his beautiful staircase, Bordeaux".

At n. 5, Cours de l'Intendance, the Acquart (de Combes) house has a monumental ground floor. Two atlantes support the balcony on the finest floor on which three neo-classical façades and two finely sculpted panels alternate. The top of the façade is finished with an impressive cornice surmounted with a balustrade. Further along, the Sarget passage which was opened in 1878. At n. 57, the Centre for Spanish Culture guards the memory of the painter Fransico Goya who spent the last years of his life here (1824-28).
In 1799-1800 at what was the Théâtre Français, and now a cinema, J. B. Dufart played with a triangular theme for its entrance on a corner, softened with a rounded peristyle and continued by the vista effect of the harsher façades.

One of the powerful atlantes supporting the balcony of the Acquart house.

The former Théâtre Français. In the distance, the Grands Hommes market.

The Grands Hommes market.

Rue Montesquieu leads to the centre of the Grands Hommes district, a circular square with radiating roads consecrated to the great philosophers, bounded by three main roads. This district, due to its shape is also called the 'Triangle'. The old market has been replaced by a shiny glass and metal construction, containing a shopping mall, which, as the day advances, provides a continuously changing play of reflections with the white and ochre of the stone façades surrounding the square.
To the east, a passage leads to the old cloister of the second Dominican Convent (17th century). Built after the revolt in 1675 and the subsequent decree given by Louis XIV to destroy the whole district, including the previous 13th century convent, in order to be able to extend the glacis of Chateau Trompette.

Chancel of Our Lady's Church

Façade of Our Lady's Church

Our Lady's Church

Place du Chapelet takes its name from the appearance of the Blessed Virgin of the Rosary to St Dominic, as shown by the central bas-relief on Our Lady's Church.
The chapel of the second Dominican Chapel until 1790, and built from 1684 to 1707, it is the work of the architect Duplessy. Its structure is a variation of St Paul's Church in Paris, but here, a pleasing transition has been arranged between the lower sections, the sides and the central avant-corps, due to the presence of a curved, cantoned wall at the top with two scrolls. The façade is very ornamented. The four statues, St Gregory (A), St Ambrose (B), St Jerome (C) and St Augustin (D) were crafted with the chisel of Prévot (1866). The rest of the façade is the work of Pierre II and Jean Berquin (1693) : a bas-relief of the Rosary (E), falling flowers and cherubs on the side pilasters and busts of the Dominican saints (Benedict XI, St Antonious, St Pious V, St Albert le Grand) on the upper level. The architectural decor is extremely varied, even using adorned pyramids.

EGLISE

The single nave, the side chapels and the sectioned gore of the apse are reminiscent of the church of Gésu in Rome. The chapels are joined by openings forming narrow side-aisles. Vaults and corbellings contribute to the plastic quality of the architecture. This was despite a decree from Louis XIV for a thin and light vault so that the building could not be used as a bastion for an attack against Chateau Trompette in case of revolt.
The light coming throught the windows is plentiful, side bays and the oculus of the chancel's cupola highlight the careful layout of the church.
Amongst the rich selection of paintings may be noted the collection painted by Brother André (G), a student of Jouvenet. It is a pictural history, with the intention being, amongst others to glorify the Dominican order. Rosary Chapel's altar piece (H) was probably the work of the Berquins in 1693. The high altar (I) is flanked by two angels and looked down on by a charming group of cherubs gathered together on a pyramid (Peru, 1751).
The sumptuous wrought iron grills by Moreau (1781), separating the chancel from the side-aisles, are dedicated to the Evangelists on the medallion ; St Luke and St Mark surmounted by the Assumption (J) on one and St Mathew and St John with the Ascension (K) on the other. Foliated scrolls, leaves,

The wide passaguays of the side-aisles, surmounted by bull's eyes provide access to the chapels where the most beautiful collection of church paintings in Bordeaux are hung. On the left, the oil painting by Brother André from 1732 of "St Raymond de Penafort". This Catalan Dominican friar, having accompanied King Aragon to Majorca, fell out of grace and was not allowed to return on the boat for Barcelona. Laying out his cloak on the sea and using his staff as a mast, he sailed miraculously over to the boat, climbed in and put back on his coat, which after six hours of 'sailing' was still dry!

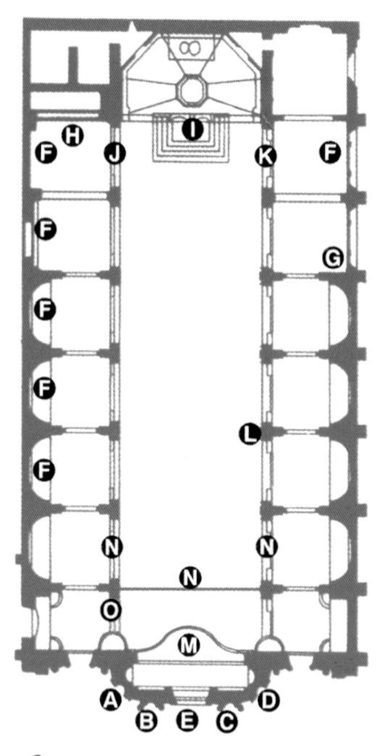

The Ascension of Christ (detail of the grills)

medallions, cornices, characters and patterns along the side sections contribute to a very high quality, shining decor with the use of gold leaf effect highlighting the lustre of certain elements to excellent effect.
The pulpit (L) in carved wood and red marble, credited to Brother Thomas, who is also responsible for the wood work of the chancel, was fitted with a new sounding-board showing the Assumption (F. Bonio), replacing the one destroyed in 1793.
The superb organ chest (M), crowned with statues of David and St Cecilia (by Brother Durel in 1781) is adorned with small angel musicians. The organ is supported on an undulating gallery with a beautiful movement

Chancel grill by Moreau. Behind it, "The Annunciation", a painting by Brother André.

The pulpit and two side chapels

created by three overhanging sections reflecting those of the first bay. The Bordeaux art of stone arrangement reaches the peak of its expression here!
The church is completed with low grills (N) and the baptismal fonts grill (O) by Faget, stained-glass windows by Villiet and Hutrel and the painted decor of the apse (1874). Impressive 18th century metalwork runs above and along the arcades of the nave. Our Lady's Church is one of the finest examples of Baroque art in Bordeaux.

Looking from the entrance, a subtle use of stereotomy can be seen on the balcony and organ loft.

North-east façade of the allées de Tourny. The Gobineau house, in the foreground, was the only building actually completed of the enormous project envisaged by Victor Louis for Place Ludovise which was abandoned.

Designed by the Intendant as a shaded walking area, the allées de Tourny occupy the site of the first Dominican Convent (1227) and where 15th and 16th century statues from the chapel were found in a ditch. The glacis of Chateau Trompette arrested all development to the north of the allées. Low, uniform houses were built on the south side, again following rules imposed for military reasons, alternating with mansard-roofed houses to break the monotony. These continue up to the semicircular square opposite the Grand Theatre. The Meyer house, built by Combes in 1796 for the Consul of Hamburg, broke away from the original restraints. The lifting of the restriction brought in a series of developments to increase the height of the houses in the following century, disrupting the harmony of the arrangement. Only the house at n. 28 and the mansard-roofed house at n. 14 remain as examples of the original model designed by Portier. In 1785, a year after the decision was taken in principle to destroy Chateau Trompette, work started on the Gobineau house (now Bordeaux's Maison de Vin) a high, 5 storey house with a ship's stem effect on the street corner. It was built according to plans drawn up by Victor Louis. It set the position of the second façade, of the allée and the later Cours du XXX Juillet on which the Tourist Office replaced the famous Café Montesquieu, frequented by Stendhal.

Place des Quinconces

Two successive Chateau Trompettes were constructed on this site ; the first after the departure of the English and the second by Vauban after the insurrection of the Fronde. Finally destroyed in 1818 (an excellent scale model is on show at the Museum of Plans and Reliefs in Paris).

A real lesson in civics, the chariot of the Triumph of the Republic from the Monument to the Girondins, facing the Grand Theatre.

The 'Triumph of Concord' from the Monument to the Girondins, facing Chartrons.

Quinconces railway station

The Rostral Columns.

Place des

Made up of a vast rectangle (A) looking over the river to the east, separated to the west by a semicircular road (B) linking the Grand Theatre to Chartrons, the place des Quinconces took its shape in the 19th century with a uniform neo-classical style elevation (C) designed by Poitevin and his colleagues, worthy successors to Percier, the Emperor's architect. Arcaded ground floor, windows in the triangular façade separated by a heavy cornice from the 2nd floor, attic windows and balustrades.
On what was the glacis, facing Chartrons, stretch uniform and less interesting façades along the length of the allées (D).
Today, the esplanade is the site for funfairs and antique fairs as well as a flower market in Spring and a ham market in Autumn which continues a long tradition.
To break the monotony of such a large expanse, Poitevin erected in 1829 two rostral colunmns facing the river, each deco-

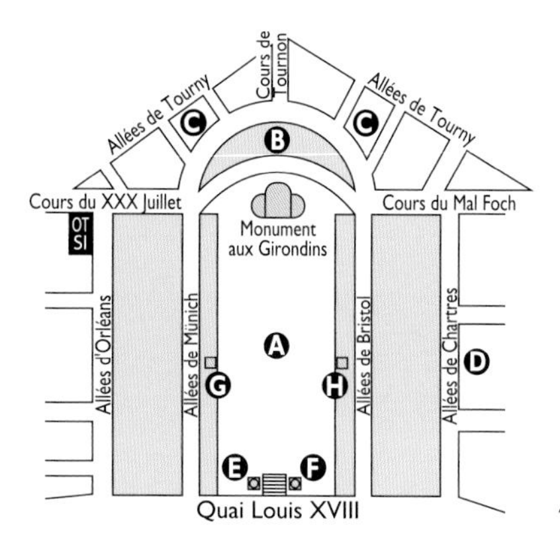

The horse-reptile with terrifying claws is striking in the realism of its head and snorting nostrils.

rated with 4 ship's bows, surmounted with the statues of Trade (E) (Mercury with his winged cap) on the town side and Industry (F) on the Chartrons side. Two colossal statues pay hommage to the literary works written in Bordeaux since 1858, Montaigne (G) and Montesquieu (H) the arduous works of Maggesi, the town sculptor.
The "Monument to the Girondins and to the Republic", both a commemorative decoration and a fountain, was erected from 1894 to 1909. The Bordelais sculptor, Dumilatre (1844-1927), despite being suspended in 1896, was the designer of the project along with the architect Victor Rich who completed the fountain. Gustave Debrie (1853-1924) claimed, rightly, the design for the sea horses, the masterpiece of this work to which he insisted on giving his name.
At the base of the column surmounted by "Liberty, setting herself free" and facing the river, the "Coq Gaulois", the Tribune, Eloquence and History are the only connections with the "Girondins", (members of the Bordeaux Parliament during the Revolution), their absence being witnessed by the empty pedestals. Facing the town, 3 women symbolise Bordeaux (in the centre) the Garonne and the Dordogne.

The Spirit of Liberty breaking itself free and soaring up from the top of the column.

Bordeaux, represented by a goddess-like woman, enthroned above two laughing water nymphs, the Garonne and the Dordogne.

"TRIOMPHE DE LA RÉPUBLIQUE"

On the Grand Theatre side, "the Triumph of the Republic", with "La République" seated on her throne exalts Work (a blacksmith), Security and Power (the lion). Three children on each side are reminders of the fundamental laws voted in at the time, "obligatory education"(on the right) and military service (on the left). A quadrige of horse-reptiles or fish are pushing into the abyss Lies carrying a mask, Vice and Ignorance.

Drawings : MM. Trillaud and Bariac.

Facing Chartrons 'the triumph of Concord'. Carrying an olive branch, 'La Concorde' protects Fraternity (a worker and a townsperson) and Abundance from which is born the prosperity of Industry and Trade (three children on the left) and the Arts (three children on the right) ; the same quadrige is preceded this time by Happiness (a cherubim riding a dolphin and a couple).

"TRIOMPHE DE LA CONCORDE"

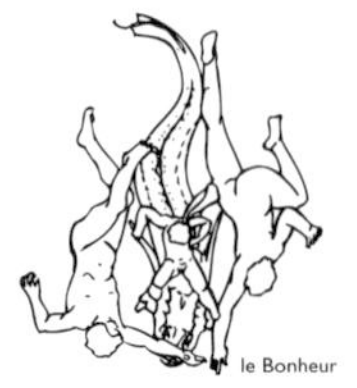

Constructed at the time of the triumphant "statuomanie", the bronzes, enhanced by the water, one of the most powerful statements made during the 3rd Republic. Removed in 1943 to be sent to the foundry, they were found intact in 1945 and the groups were put back in position in 1983.
This monument sets off the ornamentation of the square due to its size, the high quality of the bronzes in the basins and the impressive programme of iconography. It is a unique example of civic decor in an urban environment in France in the 19th century, following the embankment, you arrive at rue Ferrère, the site of the Bourse Maritime (1920), a nostalgic pseudo-Louis XV pastiche of the central block of the Bourse. At the rear are the Lainé warehouses which retain, long after their closure, the odours of coffee, cocoa, vanilla and other spices, where they were stored behind the Piranese porch.
As part of the development of the port and river banks, Deschamps who had just finished the work on the Pont de pierre, was asked to construct warehouses on an irregular plot of land. This functional architecture, with multi-purpose areas, bears the signs of a classical education, given at that time by the College of Bridges and Roads. In the same way as for the Pont de pierre, he used a stone and brick masonry technique, the only example of its systematic use in Bordeaux. The exterior walls with alternating courses of rubble and brick are not dissimilar to the technique used on the Palace of Gallienus Designed like a basilica with a two-naved hall at its centre rising up to the roof, side galleries, semicircular arches, and groined and barrel vaults over the stairways in the four corners. Today it houses the Contemporary Art Museum.
Coming back onto the quai des Chartrons, (from "chartreux", the Carthusian monks who drained the district in the Middle Ages), notice the Fenwick house with its two "observatories" which allowed the rich American Consul and merchant to follow the activities in the port. The official character of this private dwelling, built by Dufart in 1795 and restored in 1870, is underlined by the two rostrums (prows of ships) in the antique style, symbols of shipping and trade.

The Lainé Warehouse. The series of semicircular arches brings to perfection the "Piranese style" atmosphere that these premises emanate.

Quai des Chartrons, for a long time planted with trees, was in the 16th and 17th century inhabited by foreign merchants, who avoided the heavy taxes on the export of wine by being outside the town walls. Set between two buildings is the entrance to the Cité Mondiale du Vin et des Spiritueux, the work of M. Pétuaud-Létang. Built since 1991, it has a large glass wall overlooking a segment-shaped courtyard .

Further down the embankment, at n. 28-29, a middle class Bordelais built these two house with Flemish style "gables" in around 1680. They were the only Dutch homes spared after the reordering of Tourny. This aligning enables us today to consider a large number of 18th century merchants residences with their carriage entrances and wrought iron balconies (n. 39-40) They span the roads which give access to the port by arches, an example of which is that over rue Barrayre. Come back down rue Borie (n. 41) to visit the Wine Museum in a beautiful 18th century house, then wander down rue Notre-Dame, taken over by antique dealers, and the adjacent roads on which the Louis XVI style and neo-classical façades, more modest yet harmonious, conjure up the memory of the numerous labourers and craftsmen who worked for the merchants. Beautiful balconies at n. 95, 89 and 52. St Louis'church (1875) erected on the site of the Carmelite chapel retains superb examples of the work of joiners. Father Canteloup lived here (the Carmelites were early pharmacists) the inventor of melissa cordial, the famous "Carmelite Cordial"! The neo-classical chapel at n. 12-14 is the finest example of the many that were built in France during the Restoration ; constructed for the protestant community, composed mainly of rich foreign merchants. The building has a porch with a triangular façade on four Ionic columns with the only decor being an open bible in relief. Inside, a single, barrel vaulted nave.

The recently renovated Chartrons quays.

The Chartrons market (1869)

The Fenwick house, from the 18th century, with a ground floor restored by Durand in 1870, to create the 'serlian' entrance with four columns.

On arriving at the Pavé des Chartrons (Cours Xavier-Arnozan) you are met with the most impressive deceptive vista of balconies in the town, along the north side of the road that was divided and built uniformly by Laclotte from 1770 to 1780. The construction is functional, from the cellars turned into store houses to the attics where the servants lived, offices on the ground floor, drawing rooms on the finest floor and appartments on the second. The Cours de Verdun, lined with houses dating from 1760 to 1900, continues the austere Louis XVI style which has lasted despite modifications to more modern styles. This cours provides access to the Jardin Public.

The Flemish houses

Balconies on pendentives of the Pavé des Chartrons

Every spring, the "flower basket" of the "English" garden spreads its finery over the green lawns of the Jardin Public.

The Jardin Public

This large expanse designed by Tourny was originally planted with trees as a French style garden. Known as the Champ de Mars at the time of the Revolution, it was converted into a landscape garden in 1856 with all the accessories (rivers, bridges, islands) (A), and then into a botanical garden (B) with greenhouses lined with a stone gallery (C). The gallery was remodelled by d'Welles who opened up a palladian bay and decorated it with a climbing plant design. A closed terrace (D) facing the place du Champ de Mars to the south presents two elegant porches with Ionic columns and balustrades. The gates and doors (E) in wrought iron designed by Portier and manufactured by Dorse and Kanzac were repaired by the master locksmith Faget in the 19th century. The Lisleferme house (F) (1780), decorated by Cabirol, which is now the Natural History Museum was the first example of a continuity in architectural style which was to be repeated in this area for over a century. The house of the merchant Calvet is notable amongst these (currently the home of the renowned Academy of Arts and Sciences, founded by Montesquieu amongst others in the 18th century). It is an accurate imitation with balustered balconies, triangular faced quoins and the balustraded cornice which surmounts it. More strikingly, as a continuation to the Pavé des Chartrons a century later, the merchants built a row of uniformy classic style houses the whole length of the north side of the gardens, along rue d'Aviau (G).
Along rue Emile Zola are small gardens backing onto the park, in the Parisian style of Parc Monceau (H).

A flower covered mound on the support of the bridge crossing the lake in the landscaped garden.

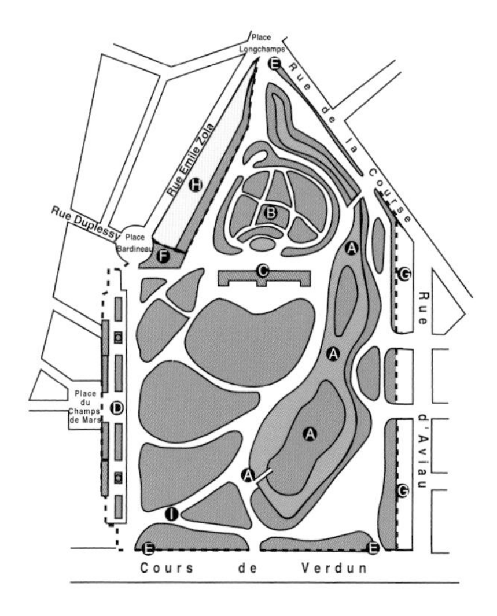

Bust of Mauriac by Zadkine.

In the Jardin Public, generations of children have watched the Guerin puppet show and, nearby, voyaged in the “Petit Mousse” pleasure boat. The most famous of these children was François Mauriac, whose bust was placed here in 1985 for the centenary of his birth.

Bas-relief decor by Cabirol in the “four seasons” room of the Lisleferme house.

In front of the colonnade, and included in the original designs for the Jardin Public, the statue of Rosa Bonheur, one of a long line of Bordelais artists and sculptors of which she is the finest.

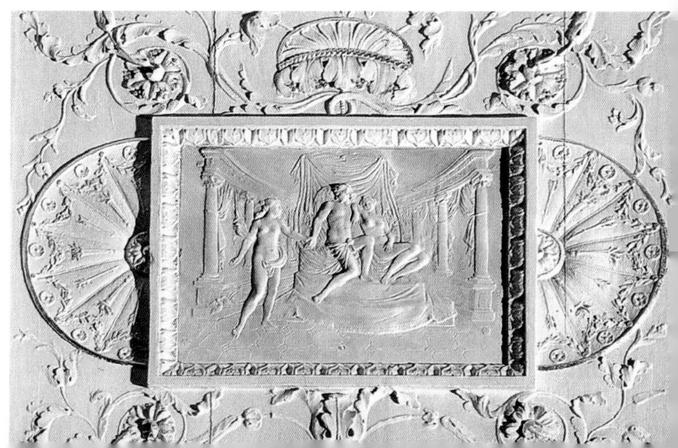

Of the Gallo-Roman amphitheatre, the Palace of Gallienus, only the enormous gateway and a few adjacent courses of the walls remain. Together with those stones incorporated into the surrounding gardens and houses, these are the last remains (apart from the foundation of the Castrum) of ancient Burdigala. According to tradition, the arena was always located outside the town's walls. Legend says that Charlemagne built it for his wife Galliene (hence rue Palais Gallien), although it actually dates from the 3rd century, when the Roman Emperor was called Gallienus !
The construction, built from thin courses of rubble and brick, had an area of about 133 by 111 m with an arena of 70 by 47 m, a standard size for this type of building. It was made up from seven elliptical crowns sectioned into 64 bays by hidden lateral walls and filled with wooden tiers supported by putlogs (horizontal wooden beams) embedded in the masonry in holes that can still be seen in the walls.

Palace of Gallienus. The arrangement of bricks on the arches, and the alternating nature of the rubble and brick in long courses in the walls, are examples of the subtle Gallo-Roman decoration that gives it a characteristic harmonious feel.

Rue Fondaudege takes you to the fountain in place Gruet, designed by the Girondin, Louis Garros (1865). The pedestal composed of three half-columns supporting the aedicule with aquatic pseudo-renaissance decor designed functionally as was the norm for fountains used for drawing water up to the 20th century. At the centre, a basin bears the plinth for the nymph personifying Audege's spring which used to supply the district.
The adjacent road, rue Victoire Américaine (named after Victoire Eynaud, who came from the Americas and who was the wife of the earthenware maker Hustin, who sold the land to Laclotte) has a long, homogenous façade, with balconies on consoles running the full length of the road on the first floor and without decoration, an early indication of the concern for function.

In rue Huguerie, from 1782 onwards, Lhote built series of similar, uniform houses with sober ironwork balconies, and others, still more severe in the road which bears his name.
Place Tourny, designed by the Intendant, to whom the statue pays hommage, marks, as elsewhere, the rectilinear nature of the town's principal roads. Originally it completed the small oval square of the "allées", with the low houses of the same arrangement.
The de la Marine house (n. 9) built in 1758 and decorated by Francin to be used as a convent for the Religious of the Faith (Dames de la Foi). The nearby Nairac house, the most spoilt work of Victor Louis, has a main courtyard surrounded by low wings with half-floors from which emerge the top of the very refined architectonic design of the main portion of the building.
The Dublan house, 55 Cours Clémenceau, designed by Lhote, opens up to a vaulted passageway leading to a central, circular entrance hall surmounted with a panelled cupola, an access point to all the apartments. Next to it, the elevation of the Journu-Aubert house (a rich family of ship-owners) reflects that of the îlot Louis with balconies on scalloped consoles. The house at n. 35 is decorated with a 'serlian' three-sided bay on columns surmounted with a semicircular arcade.

Fountain in Place Charles Gruet.

What was the place d'Armes in front of the Fort du Hâ, and now renamed as place de la République, has been limited by the façades of St André's Hospital (1826) then by the palais de Justice (1828). In 1912, the Monument to the Gironde Militiamen (volunteers) was erected by the followers of the "Revanche" movement after the Franco-Prussian War of 1870.

Founded in 1390 by Vital Carles, St André's Hospital has just celebrated its 600th anniversary. This 'visionary founder of the modern spirit of medicine advocated that patients should be "looked after" and not merely sheltered or excluded.
The new hospital took the place of a seminary and an elm-lined avenue, the name of which is associated with the Bordeaux 'La Fronde' which held its meetings there in the 17th century It is a very large collection of buildings comprising a large courtyard surrounded by galleries and smaller courtyards "for the well-being of patients" who are bathed in the sun's rays. On each side of the peristyle, preceded by majestic steps, the wide avant-corps leads to the square reserved for the services. Above the porch stands the square-based dome of the chapel. The whole construction is in a strictly functional, neo-classical style typical of Jean Burguet.

The large, arcaded main courtyard of St André's hospital.

Interior staircase from a house in Bordeaux.

In the same style but more restrained, on the other side of the square, the Palais de Justice, designed by the Bordelais Thiac, occupies a vast rectangular area with the steps finishing at a colonnade, surmounted with 3 arcotere gables, opening out into the disproportionate room of the "pas-perdus". The staircase is cantoned with the corners of the square by two blind avant-corps with solid foundation masses. On the roof, four statues of famous magistrates stand out, carved by Maggesi, the town sculptor; Malesherbes and d'Aguesseau to the west and Montesquieu and l'Hospital to the east.
On Cours d'Albret (n. 91) St. Marc's house is one of the best examples of neo-palladian architecture in Bordeaux. Admirers of turn of the century art can make a detour to place Amédée Larrieu ("champion of democratic ideas in the second Empire") where the fountain, designed by Vernet and constructed thanks to a legacy, symbolises Bordeaux related allegorically to the wine industry. In 1901 a market was added with a "stimulating" decor of ironwork and two fountains. Around the rue de Pessac stretches a district of "échoppes" - single-storey houses typical of popular architecture in Bordeaux.

Long before the 3rd Republic, the Bordelais Thiac built the "last great display of neo-classicism", Greek and Roman, as it should be, for the law courts (in French, le Temple de Thémis, who was the goddess of Justice). To accentuate the austerity, four stone magistrates, sitting on the terrace, seem to be watching over the proceedings.

The coffered cupola of the peristyle of the house of St Mark.

Fountain in Place Amédée Larrieu.

The Labour Exchange (Bourse de Travail) for which d'Welles was made responsible, was decorated by talented, mainly local artists. The building is in the form of a double trapezium ; at the rear the Union headquarters and offices, at the front, the hall, foyers, conference rooms etc. The entrance doors in wrought iron represent the town's trade guilds. Above, a large twelve-bayed window dominates the façade leaving room on the left for a bas-relief by Janniot, "An allegory of Bordeaux and the activities which keep it alive", personified by its monuments, ships, vineyards etc. and crowned by the town's three crescents symbol. The hall staircase leads to two completely painted foyers (frescoes in places).

The "échoppes", originally the rural houses of the Bordelais, were adapted to the 19th century for the working classes (craftsmen, labourers etc.). These people were originally wine growers, who on working in the city, brought with them this style of housing. On one floor, it contains a side corridor (single échoppe) or a central one (double échoppe) giving onto the rooms, including a scullery opening into the garden. The fronts often bear simple elements of decor to reflect the modest desire of the occupant for social climbing!

On the right, Caverne has illustrated the glory of Bordeaux's architecture and de Buzan the past of Bordeaux. On the left, a wine by Roganeau (1883 - 1973) depicts Apollo in his chariot amongst wine pickers and uncouth drinkers ; next to it, the more educational eulogy to the pine forests of the Landes by Bégaud, a major source of wealth for the resin tappers of the time. The decoration of the conference rooms (authorization required for access) was conferred to the best artist amongst those working on the building, Jean Dupas (1882-1964) of world renown who designed "The Glory of Bordeaux", "Civilisation" and "Culture" and who completed during the war the collection of paintings in grey that decorate the north wall of the room. The port and shipping are illustrated by Marco Pillot.

The "Glory of Bordeaux" and a detail of the grey work by Jean Dupas.

A parish church since 1175, St Eulalie has three naves with wide bays, a narthex to the west together with more modern additions which are difficult to accurately determine due to the alterations that took place in the 14th and 20th centuries. The furniture is particularly interesting. In St Clair's chapel, the grill which was made by Blaise Charlut, the protecting saints against the plague, St Sebastian and St Roch, are worshipped. St Roch's staff dating from the 16th century originates from the Carmelite church, destroyed during the revolution as well at the beautiful lectern which came later. The wooden statue of St Roch, recently polychromed, with his clothes, shoes and the styling of his face may be likened to the characters from the 15th century Deposition of the Cross at St Michel. According to popular tradition, an oil painting from 1666 of St Jeanne de Valois by Mazoyer.
At the rear of the church (rue P.L. Lande), all that remains in reasonable condition is the classical façade of the 17th century chapel of the Ladies of St Joseph. The old "Maison de la Miséricorde" (literally the House of Mercy) was a rescue home for unfortunate women in the 19th century, to become the centre for Cultural Affairs, hidden in the walls of the cloisters of the convent church of the Annunciation, completed in about 1530. The chapel houses an impressive entombement, retaining its medieval iconography, but with the classicism and beauty of the figures and faces which are similar to those of Biron Castle, held in New York.
In rue Lalande, only the dome of the cupola of the very old St Côme amphitheatre remains of the former faculty of medicine as a reminder of its architectural style which is quite unusual for the 18th century.

St Eulailie's church : the staff of St Roch.

Bas-relief from the "Allegory of Bordeaux and the activities which keep it alive".

The consecration of the convent of Our Lady of Mercy seems in total harmony with the atmosphere of this entombement.

Following rue Sainte-Catherine, you arrive at the synagogue dating from 1882 and built in a district inhabited by middle class jews and craftsmen descended from the marans. Close by is the Carmelite convent, the home of the first University to which the Madelene college was added in the 17th century and run by the Jesuits, which is today the Montaigne College.

Place de la Victoire

Formerly Place d'Aquitaine, it retains the traces of Portier's unfinished project which involved placing two rectangular squares on either side of the gate, one on the town side and the other at the arrival point of the road from Spain. The square was to have been enclosed with low houses having arcades on the ground floor, a further storey with balconies (replaced by handrails), and a French style mansard curb roof with attic windows. The large number of original buildings contrasting with the height of houses built later, together with fairly random modification to the area in the 19th and 20th centuries have meant that the vast and harmonious design was never carried out

The porte d'Aquitaine, the work of Portier, dedicated to the young Duke of Aquitaine who had just been born, replaced the old porte St Julien, destroyed in 1744 and located further to the south. Built from 1753-56, it joins the road to Spain and the south of France with rue St Julien (rue Ste-Catherine). It stands between two squares with on the south facing side, twinned Tuscan columns with a ringed appearance to harmonize with the embossed decoration on the gate. The construction is surmounted by a façade decorated by Francin of the

La Porte d'Aquitaine, Place de la Victoire and the column by the sculptor Ivan Theimer in hommage to vineyards and wine.

The interior of the synagogue, devastated during the second world war has been refitted with new furniture.

Entrance to the St François house. Keystones, caryatids, pattern on the balcony, design of the ironwork, woodwork of the door, arcade - all competing in a mixture of styles reinterpreted by the eclecticism of the 19th century.

arms of France, carried by two sailors. Facing the town, Tuscan pilasters support the façade on which the arms of Bordeaux emerge from a large shell decorated with fruit, flowers, sickles, bell-hooks and barrels symbolic of the resources which have made the town prosper. The gate like so many others, has lost the narrow entrance gates for pedestrians, openings in the side walls which closed off access to the town.
Rue du Mirail, which led pilgrims in the Middle Ages, from the route de Toulouse to St James hospital (traces of whose 15th century chapel may be observed at no. 10) and from there to the present Cours Victor-Hugo where the sarcophagus was discovered in 1968 of an 8th century pilgrim wearing a necklace of scallop-shells.
At n. 22 rue du Mirail, the St François house, built around 1850 by Audebert in a neo-Baroque style and enclosing the courtyard of the former Estrade house (1655) would be almost a pastiche, if it were not for its size. Nearby a very old house at n. 26. The old Puységur house (n. 36), now a private school, built in a Louis XIII mannerist style faces the Martin or de Razac house at n. 53, built around 1610 with a beautiful doric columned entrance.

Reconstructed in about 1748 in a classical Louis XV style, influenced by Gabriel, the Leberthon house (n. 31-35) has a Louis XVI style porch.
At the corner of cours Victor Hugo and rue Pilet stands one of the last half-timbered houses with crossbraces in the form of the cross of St André. Up to 1844 at the entry to rue des Faures was the "gunsmiths house", a construction of the same type with a shop on the ground floor surmounted with a porch roof. The narrowness of the roads and the concern over public health put pressure on the aldermen, from the 16th century, to abolish porch roofs, however the decisions were often not implemented for many years. Rue des Faures, formerly the rue des Armuriers (gunsmiths), and also known for its goldsmiths, used to echo to the sound of blacksmiths'hammers, leads to place Saint-Michel, the site of Bordeaux's flea market and where the spire and church of St Michel stands.

Half-timbered house on rue Pilet.

In the 19th century, there were still many half-timbered house such as this which disappeared during the urban development undertaken at that time.

St Michel : at the foot of the bell-tower, almost completely remodelled by P. Abadie, the spire watches over the flea market which used to be held in the Mériadeck district before its demolition. The church is listed as world heritage as part of the Saint Jacques de Compostelle pilgrim paths.

EGLISE SAINT-MICHEL

Founded in 1174, the parish is one of craftsmen and tradesmen associated with the port, of seamen and bargemen, as the names of the roads recall. Started in the 14th century, the church was finished two centuries later, with a separate bell-tower, in the same way as St André that it exceeds in terms of size. Being dedicated to St Michel, the patron saint of the kings of France assured it a share of the extravagances of Louis XI. The architectrual decor of "crockets" and "pennants" indicate the persistance of the gothic tradition, true also for the fittings, up to the end of the 16th century. The major repair work required after the collapse of the chancel vaults in 1693 has made it difficult to undertake an accurate analysis of the monument.

The West Door (A) surmounted by a rose window is traditional. On the tympanum, the "Adoration of the Magi and the Sheperds" (16th century) is shown in two monographs in vertical panels. The South Door (B) remodelled in 1876 has retained an "Apparition to St Michel on Mont-Gargan" credited to Cabirol. In the apse, a large bay opens above a gallery crowning the three apsidal chapels. The north side (C) has irregular lines due to the necessity to celebrate mass after the destruction of the first church. The North Door (D) is a blend of Gothic traditions with the early Renaissance style of angels on the arch mouldings of the tympanum split in two vertical panels on which a landscape vista monograph forms a frame for the scenes of the offering up of Abel and the sacrifice of Abraham. Above the Blessed Virgin and St John, the Trinity, and the Annunciation. The most interesting works are those of the prophets on the pied-droits, notably David with his lyre. The tormented faces of the old people is particular to Bordeaux, and evokes the Burgundian workshops of the 15th century, contrasted with the young prophets'normal facial features next to David. It is also the first time since the Middle Ages that a name, Julien Rochereau, has been associated with a work of art. In the medieval tradition, he adopted the new style (Renaissance) introduced by François I on his return from Italy.

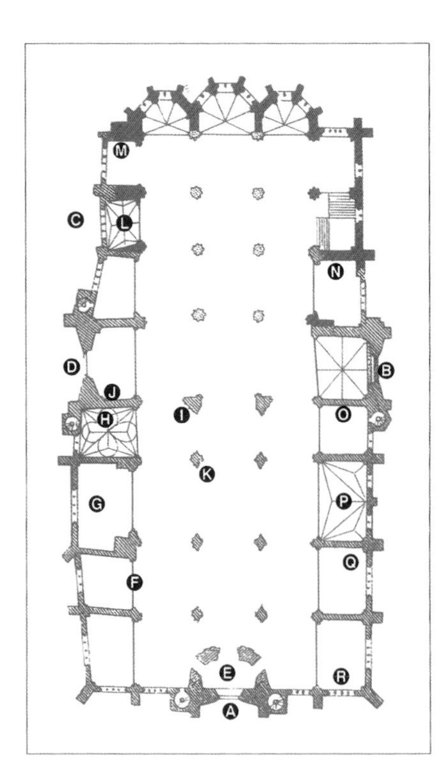

Detail on the north tympanum : the young man and King David (D).

Detail of the mannerist altar piece of St Joseph's Chapel : St Catherine, the Blessed Virgin and Sainte Barbara (H).

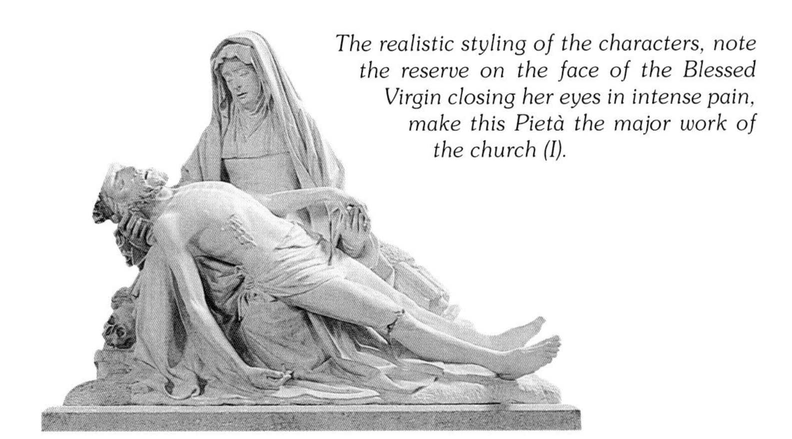

The realistic styling of the characters, note the reserve on the face of the Blessed Virgin closing her eyes in intense pain, make this Pietà the major work of the church (I).

The wide hall with three naves, all of the same height, similar to the open chapels in each bay, culminating in the three apsidal chapels of the apse are reminiscent of the hall churches of the 15th century. In the 18th century the chapels were closed off by a beautiful series of wrought iron grilles. The organ and its chest supported by the Alary loft (E) were constructed at that time. The grill of St Elisabeth's chapel (F) is the work of Dumaine. In the neighbouring one (G) can be found the tombstones of tradesmen. The rib vaults and undoubtedly the large scale altar piece of St Joseph's chapel (H) where St Catherine, the Blessed Virgin and St Barbera, protectress of young girls, are displayed, are examples of the mannerist style of the time. A century older, a series of eight English alabaster panels have been mounted on the altar. The Pietà (I), a desperate Mary and a stiffened Christ seemingly sliding to his knees, are reminders of the Bourbonnais School which started to influence artistic trends at the end of the 15th century.

The interior tympanum of the North Doors (D) depicts the temptation of Adam and Eve and their explusion from Paradise on two vertical registers. Under a flamboyant arcature, the Ecce Homo. In the west window (J) the highly coloured elements of the 16th century in one of the stained glass windows show the angel musicians surmounting four panels of the Blessed Virgin and the Magi. The aerial bombing in 1940 destroyed almost all the 16th century windows, which were replaced in 1950, with windows that try to recreate the luminous effects of stained glass windows. In the triforium there is still a Madonna and child and a St Michel (K). The surmounted pulpit of St Michel (L) was fitted in 1753.
St Sepulchre's chapel (M): a touching Deposition of the Cross with the characters created from a 'pallid' material creating a dramatic effect.

The Deposition of the Cross, from 1493 (M).

Detail of the st Joseph's chapel

Saint-Michel's church in the 19th century

The only virtually complete example of 16th century stainedglass in the de Mons Chapel. St Parenté (the three Mary's) surmounted by the tree of Jesse (the geneology of Jesus) (S).

St Ursula, according to legend, was murdered at the same time as the massacre of the eleven thousand virgins, by the Huns in Cologne (R).

St Jacques'chapel (N) : a beautiful Renaissance altar dedicated to the Blessed Virgin.
St Apollonie's chapel (patron saint of dentists) : an 18th century Spanish Crucifixion (O)
Montuzets chapel (P) has retained its vault and is usually the site for a Batanchon Annunciation.
St Agnes ' chapel (Q) : a beautiful 18th century chandelier (Cabirol) near a Louis XIII altar piece consecrated to the Madonna and child.
In the last chapel (R) dedicated to St Catherine, a limestone St Ursula, with a renovated head, shelters under her cloak the 11000 virgins, a king, an emperor, a pope a cardinal and his bishops. The softness of the faces of the piece is reminiscent of the "détente" style (around 1500) and the characters in the foreground show the influence of the theme of the "Virgin of Mercy".

The spire of the nearby bell-tower of St Michel has stood since the 16th century, the most popular symbol of the city, which even today, may be seen illuminated in the evening from the Pont de pierre. A masterpiece of the 15th century, the ruined spire and its base were renovated by Abadie from 1861-69. Built on the ancient cemetry, the high octagonal stand supports the 114 m high spire. Only the underground chapel which allows access to the ossuary remains of the 15th century construction. In 1990 the famous "real mummies" were taken away, which had been frightening tourists from the romantics up to modern times.

St Michel was a popular, colourful and even turbulent district. During the insurrection of La Fronde, it supported the Prince of Condé and later, in 1675 provided strong support to the rebellion. As a punishment Louis XIV nearly had the bell-tower destroyed. Since the Middle Ages it was a district of craftsmen and seamen : rue Carpenteyre where the heavy timber carpenters worked, and the wet coopers on rue de la Fusterie. The latter street, lined with tall 18th and 19th century residences has retained two beautiful Renaissance houses. One of these (n. 35) houses a gallery of shops with 17th century diamond pointed archstones, a rather "luxurious" decoration often used for this type of building in Bordeaux. The other (n. 31) is surprising in terms of its size and consequence as well as the height of its imposing gables on which scrolled keystones ornament the windows. It is one of the rare examples of the large stone houses that used to be widespread in this district, and which were homes for the rich middle-class tradespeople. Opposite (n.34), a tall house (18th to 19th century) has an interesting ironwork balcony resting on three pendentives.
The quarter's craftsmen used to find the wood which they needed close to hand since it was unloaded just below the church on the banks of the Garonne from special barges (arriving from the river and its tributaries further upstream and usually destroyed once the cargo was unloaded). It was also an area of netmakers where seamen and bargemen came to stock up with the equipment necessary for fishing and shipping from the shipchandlers of the time.

From the crenellations of Château Trompette, observors could admire the Tourny façade and moored ships, even further away than St Michel. (Painting by J. Vernet, Musée de la Marine).

On Quai des Salinières, the lively market disappeared to make way for the access to the Pont de Pierre and the requirements of traffic. There, on the embankment, in 1788, on the site of an old fountain, stood a fluted column decorated with imitation bunches of roses in the pre-Romantic style of the period. Moved in the 19th century, the fountain supplied the boats as well as the district after great problems in making the water drinkable. The water still flows today.

The Grave fountain.

The Bordeaux waterfront along the river continues to the other end of the Quai de la Grave in a uniform style, as imagined by Tourny. Away from the river, the façades witness his desire to continue this project of uniformity right back to St Croix, but also his failure. The Porte de la Monnaie (1752-1758) with its size and sober decoration of niches and embossed work surmounted by a triglyph frieze seems very modest in relation to the other gates on the main artery roads. To the rear, la Monnaie (the Mint) remained in the 1750 building bearing its name until 1801.

A polychrome Christ from the end of the 15th century.

THE CHURCH OF

The first sanctuary would have been built on the site of a Gallo-Roman necropolis. The sarcophagus of its founder, a certain Mommolénus (643 BC) has been saved. Donations enabled the Benedictines to build the first church (10th - 11th century) and to accord themselves the status as a Sanctuary. The establishment of a large area of real estate brought them long-lasting wealth. The religious order of St Maur succeeded them, building the beautiful, classic 17th century buildings that adjoin on the right, the school of Fine Art that we can see today.

The irregular decoration of the walls of the nave, on the outside, are the only remains of the first church which had few bays, and a wooden roof. The vaulted apse and the 12th century transept were followed by the pillars of the nave which are now covered. Around 1150, the vaults were placed after reinforcing the walls, and the west front was raised, renovated in 1860 by Abadie who added a bell-tower, symmetrical to the original Romanesque one to the south (A).

Inside the primitive decor has been spoilt by subsequent work after 1860. All that remains of the original work are some Moorish fittings, such as the organ chest (B) from 1748, the woodcarvings of the sachristy and a marble altar in the apsidal side chapel (C), a torch-carrying angel (D) and a rococo console in gilded wood (E) made for the church in the 17th century.

Of the Romanesque sculpture, there remains :

- eight medallions of the founders holding a church in their hands (F)
- the high quality capitals of the pillars of the transept crossing (G)
- Daniel in the lions' den helped by Habacuc (H)
- Jesus found by his parents in the company of the elders of the church (I)
- The sacrifice of Abraham (J) and several other more ordinary capitals.

The south transept seems to have been shortened with the start of the ribbed vault and cut short at the same level as the gabled wall (K).

The collection of classical paintings come from the destroyed church of the Capucin friars. In the north aisle is the tomb of St Mommolénus (L) who exorcised the possessed and was highly venerated, as indicated by the painting by G. Cureau. Further along a classic St Anthony (M), then a large oil painting from 1698, reminiscent of a mixture of Poussin and clumsiness, an exaltation to St François-Xavier from 1740 (N).

The apse of the church of St Croix can now be appreciated with an overall view of the Moorish buildings to the bell-tower added in the 19th century.

St Croix

Several votive offerings were made in this district near to the port: one can be seen in a 19th century naive painting (O) in which the Blessed Virgin appears above a sinking boat "a token of respect from Mrs Duprat and her children".
The large figure of Christ with a bald head (P), 3.90 m high in lime wood dates without doubt from the third quarter of the 15th century (an emotional face and polychromed with clots of blood on the chest). Did he once wear a wig like certain Spanish crucifixion figures?
Finally, St Maur (Q) founder of the religious order, by G. Cureau and dating from 1647, hanging from St Mammolin and raising up a miraculously healed person, as is expected at any time as a result of the prayers being offered!

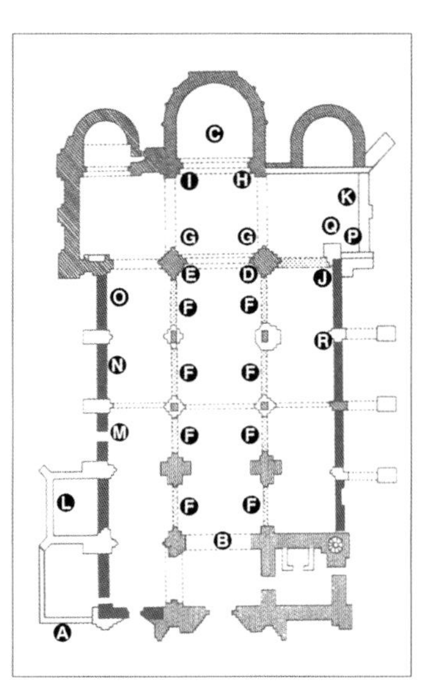

The west front before its restoration by Abadie in 1860.

The construction of the Regional Conservatory in 1980, an enormous yet functional work built by Messrs Perrier and Mothe, has left space, on the side facing the town for the creation of a large square which highlights the elements which surround it (ancient rampart, Rococco fountain, monastic buildings) and above all, clears the view of the church of St Croix so that the Romanesque apse, can be observed more easily with its two apsidal chapels with their typically saintangais appearance (from a province of France), despite the inevitable restoration work on the apse.
The fountain of St Croix, in Rococco style, was erected in 1735 backing onto the remains of the 14th century rampart, a roughly dressed agglomerated wall of rubble and small bricks and surmounted by a walkway with crenellations. The statue was designed as nymph with aquatic decor ; the central concave niche houses an aedicule in scallops at the centre of the cornice. The "water chandeliers" enthroned on the pilasters and at the bottom of the triple revolution stairs leading to the basin.

The fountain of St Croix, resting against the 14th century ramparts, the remains of which can be seen on the right.

Château Descas, the model for a number of later châteaux, built in a vineyard at the end of the last century.

The quai de Paludale is a reminder of the marshy origin of the district ("palus" means marsh in old French) and the naval shipyards which were the pride of Bordeaux in the 18th century. In 1893, the architect Ricard built a house here in the historicist style ; decorated by Pompon, in effect a chateau of impressive size for the merchant Descas. The latter had his offices in his wine stores one of which was located, up until its recent renovation in the remains of the 17th century Manufacture hospital.

The **Gare St Jean** (1888-1900) built by Toudoire and Choron replaced the "wooden station" of the Southern France Company and was built at the point of arrival of the Eiffel bridge (1859) linking the Southern France Company network to that of the Orléans company, whose station can still be seen on the other side of the river near the Pont de Pierre. The ornamentation of the long façade was undertaken by the Bordelais sculptors Beylard (St Jean block) and by Lerous (Terminus block).
The metal superstructures of the station concourse blends traditional architecture with that of the embankment, to create one of the prides of rail architecture which, when it was built, had the largest station concourse in the world, (1898), surprising its contemporaries by its size. The quality of the stonework, the proportions, its functional appearance and the ease of use for the traveller (outshining Orsay station in terms of its architecture and St Lazarre in terms of access) have made it an important monument to rail architecture, indeed a station worthy of a capital, as was the intention of the Pereire brothers, who hoped to regain for Bordeaux thanks to its railway, the splendour of the Golden Century. A series of problems during its construction and after delayed its inauguration until ...1987! the date on which the final restoration work was completed.
Taking the bus up the **Cours de la Marne**, offers a view of the Naval Health School at no. 145 which has taken over from what was the lunatic asylum, and next to it, Gustave Eiffel college (n. 141-3) in the former premises of the workhouse, built by Combes (who promoted the neo-classical style in the region) in 1808 on the site of the old plague hospital, built outside the walls of the town in 1550.

The Terminus house, placed in front of the long façade of the Gare Saint-Jean.

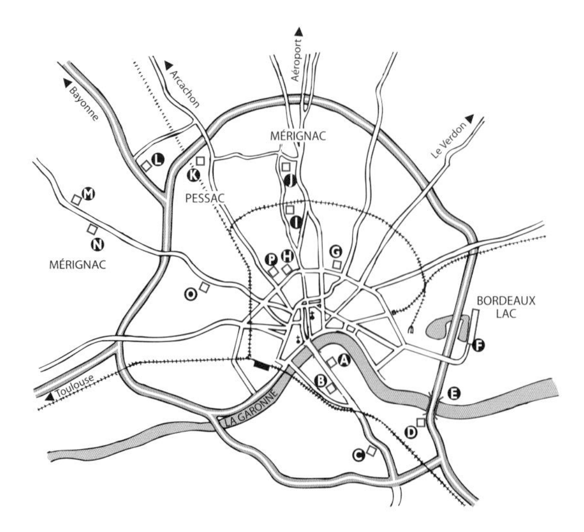

A Eglise Ste Marie
B Maison cantonale
C Parc Palmer
D Résidence d'été des arche vêques
E Pont d'Aquitaine
F Bordeaux Lac
G Parc Bordelais
H Parc des Sports
I Maison d'Arlac
J Tour de Veyrines
K Cité Fruges
L Etablissement des Monnaies
M Prieuré de Cayac
N Serres Gustave Eiffel
O Château Peixotto
P Ciné-théâtre Girondin

For certain sites (I,J and K) a detailed road map would be useful.

Around Bordeaux

Bordeaux's first bridge, the Pont de Pierre, enabled the Garonne to be crossed only as recently as 1822. Intended for this site for many years, despite the power of the currents which carried away the first piers built under Napoleon I, it was only at the time of the Restoration, and thanks to the dedication of a prefect, a minister and a merchant, that the engineer Claude Deschamps was able to put forward the plan for a bridge in brick and stone. The double advantage of his design was the provision of a gallery in its structure which enabled the whole length to be accessed and reducing the weight at the same time.

For the first time in France, a diving bell was brought over from England in order to construct a series of wooden squares on the river bed to hold the stone bedding. Instead of attacking the piers the mud carried by the current reinforced them. The laying of the last stone was the occasion of a great festival in August 1821.

Crossing the Pont de Pierre, from the Quai de Queyries to the Bastide and thanks to a meander in the river, the

St Mary's Church, erected by P. Abadie in the Roman-historicist style of the 19th century. Vaguely similar to Sacré-Coeur in Paris which Abadie also built. It is characterised by the use of cupolas and skylights.

The Canton House, with its volumes, its brick and stonework decoration, its raised gables adorned with finials and its "belfry" style clock, recall the architecture of the north and east of France. Its appearance here is suprising.

whole historic waterfront of the town can be taken in at a glance.
From left to right, the town's development can be followed : the small bell-tower of St Pierre's church locates the former Roman port, the Grosse Cloche and the high spire of St Michel are reminders of the medieval town and the façades of the embankment and the Bourse evoke the splendour of the Golden Age. Outside these limits (from Place des Quinconces and Chartrons one side and Château Descas and the station on the other extends the 19th century urban development which continued into the 20th century in concentric ellipses from the embankment : the ramparts, around the town, then the boulevards and today the ring road.
Following Avenue Thiers takes you past St Mary's church (A) to arrive at the Cantonal House (B) of the Bastide (rue des Nuits) built in the Art Nouveau style from 1913 to 1926 to enclose a multi-purpose complex (conferences, performances, library, offices, the Justice of the Peace) where the decor produces its effect from the combination with the diversity of materials (stone, brick, iron, wood, mosaic). Certain elements (geometric sculptures, ironwork) show aspects of the new Art Deco style. Along avenue Thiers, the old road to Paris during the urbanization of the Bastide, you climb to the hills, the former site of the country houses of the rich Bordelais, one of which is open to the public, the Parc Palmer (G), with its bizarre quasi neo-classical style. Passing through Cenon, and near Lormont (a picturesque old village) take the autoroute in the direction of Bordeaux-Lac.
Just before crossing the Garonne, you can catch a glimpse on the left of the old summer residence (D) of the archbishops of Bordeaux since the 14th century. The river is crossed via the Pont d'Aquitaine (1967), an elegant structure over 50 m above water level (E).

The Pont d'Aquitaine, Bordeaux's third bridge is of the suspension type and modelled on the one at Tancarville. Raised 53 metres above the river and with a roadway of 580 metres, to which the access is via a long inclined viaduct over a kilometre long.

Passing the extensive Exhibition Centre complex of Bordeaux-Lac (F) on the right, return towards the centre of Bordeaux, then take the boulevard which joins the "barrières" (once the offices for the collection of tolls). At the barrière du Medoc, avenue Carnot leads to the 22 ha Parc Bordelais (G), a gift to the town from a 19th century benefactor, now the centre of the Bordeaux Cauderan residential district. Just after the barrière d'Ornano, the Parc des Sports (H) is a complex built by J. d'Welles and R. Jourde from 1933-38. The impressive monumental arch over the entrance refers immediately to antiquity, with a hint of Mussolinian architecture.

The simplified forms and the clearly defined volumes are reminiscent of the architecture and paintings of Chirico. The stadium is suprising, with a succession of cantilevered vaults, stretching out over the void with force and elegance. Unfortunately these have been altered to increase the capacity of the stadium. Four, large, ceramic vases, decorated with a mosaic in an antique style, revised and altered to the style of the 30's, the work of R. Buthaud, welcome the spectators as they arrive. They display naked athletes with muscled physiques. Amongst them, Hercules carrying a club strengthens the link with antiquity.
Following round the hospital complex, along avenue des Eyquems as far as

Two of the four large vases by R. Buthaud, decorated with mosaics by Foscato from the 30's.

The d'Arlac Square House : built just before the Revolution in 1792 in the Palladian style, it is mirrored by the White House in Washington.

Mérignac, the Carrée d'Arlac house (I) is one of the most famous works undertaken during the Golden Age in the outskirts of Bordeaux. Built around 1786-89 by A. Roché for the Portugese banker Peixotto, it comprises, based on the White House in Washington, a Circular Room, constructed in this case on two levels and opening into a cupola. Further along, "La Tour de Veyrines" (J) can be observed, the keep and entrance to a chateau probably built around 1300, to be later converted into a chapel. It used to belong to the mayor and aldermen of Bordeaux, the Barons of Veyrines.
Avenue Bon-Air leads to the "cité Frugès" (K) on rue Le Corbusier, the work of Le Corbusier commissioned by the industrial businessman, Frugès, a cultivated and avant-garde man. On the other side of the Rocade (ring road) on Voie Romaine, is the Etablissement des Monnaies, which may be visited, and is the only coin foundry operating in France.
Beyond Gradignan, on the main road, you reach Cayac Priory (M), the remnants of the old, Middle Age pilgrim hospital on the route to St Jacques de Compostelle. In the gardens of the Town Hall, the greenhouse has been re-erected (N), the work being originally designed by Gustave Eiffel for the Universal Exhibition in Paris in 1878.

The greenhouse at the Town Hall. The work of Gustave Eiffel's workshop.

The priory welcomed sick or tired pilgrims on the way to Compostelle. This building, restored in the 17th century bears the date of the assault by the Duke d'Epernon during the Insurrection of the Fronde, in 1649.

Returning to Bordeaux along cours de la Libération offers the chance to see, on the right, the 18th century Peixotto chateau, which has become Talence Town Hall (O), and the wrought iron gate of the new faculty of Sciences and arts. Next to the barrière de Pessac, the façade of the "Ciné-Théâtre Girondin" (P) is a reminder of the fashion among the not-so-adventurous townspeople for a range of variety acts performed before an audience of regulars in rooms such as this.

The alloy foundry used to make coins.

The façade of the former Ciné-Théâtre Girondin near the Barrière de Pessac. In the 20's, there were a fair number of these halls, where a variety of performances alternated, cinema, theatre, reviews, music hall.

Musée d'Aquitaine 20 cours Pasteur
Tél : 05 56 01 51 00 Open every day except Mondays and Public holidays, from 10 am to 6 pm.
A history museum (archeology, ethnography) covering the history of the five departments in the Aquitaine region from prehistory to the present. Collections from ancient civilisations (Egyptian, Greek) and from other continents. An introduction to Bordeaux and the region. Working displays, library, bookshop.

Musée des Beaux-Arts 20 cours d'Albret
Tél : 05 56 10 20 56 Open every day except Tuesdays and Public holidays, from 10 am to 6 pm..

Collections of very old pictures and series of Italian, Dutch and Flemish paintings from the 17th century (Giordano, Brueghel, Rubens ..). Also French painters (Delacroix, Odilon Redon ..).

CapcMusée d'Art Contemporain
Entrepôt 7 rue Ferrère
Tél : 05 56 00 81 50 Open every day except Mondays, from 11 am to 7 pm, Wednesdays from 11 am to 10 pm).

A programme of exhibitions of works belonging to the museum, library, displays concerning styles, music, theatre etc.

Musée des Arts Décoratifs
Hôtel de Lalande, 39 rue Bouffard
Tél : 05 56 00 72 53 Open every day except Tuesdays and Public holidays, from 2 pm to 6 pm.
Three storeys of rooms and corridors filled with collections of earthenware, porcelain, miniatures, jewellery, furniture, glassware, coats of arms, ironwork etc., a large part of which is made in Bordeaux.

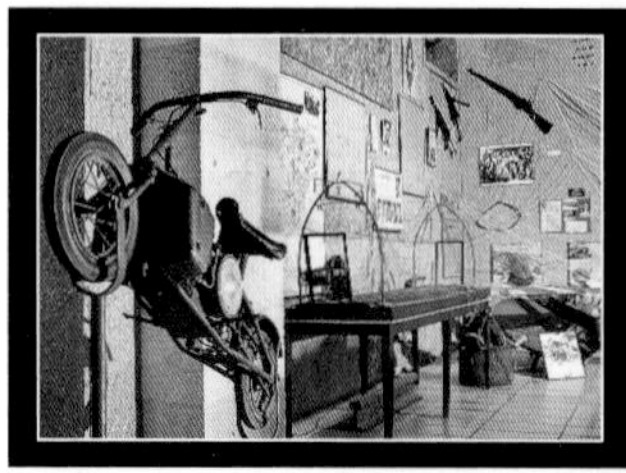

Centre National Jean-Moulin
place Jean-Moulin
Tél : 05 56 79 66 00 Open every day except Saturdays, Sundays and Public holidays, from 2 pm to 6 pm.

Collections from the 2nd World War (1939-45), the Resistance, Deportation, The Free French Force with original documentation and objects.

arc en rêve centre d'architecture bordeaux
Entrepôt 7 rue Ferrère F-33000
Tél. 05 56 52 78 36
info@arcenreve.com www.arcenreve.com
Open every day except Mondays, from 11am to 6pm.
Wednesday nocturnal till 8pm. Guided visits on appointment.

Muséum d'Histoire Naturelle
5 place Bardineau (Jardin Public)
Tél. : 05 56 48 26 37
Open every day except Tuesdays, from 2 pm to 5.30 pm (until 6 pm from the 16th of June to the 15th of September).

Collections from the five continents : mammals, birds, fish, reptiles, butterflies, minerals, fossils etc.

Musée National des Douanes
1 place de la Bourse
Tél. : 05 56 48 82 82 Open every day except Mondays, Christmas Day and New Year's Day, from 10 am to 12 and 1:30 pm to 6 pm from the 1st of April to the 30th of September (and to 5 pm from the 1st of October to the 31st of March).

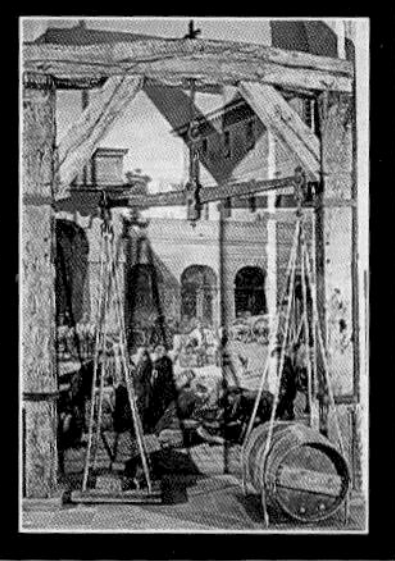

The history of the Customs Service and the tasks it is required to carry out, through uniforms, paintings, objects seized, instruments, etc.

Cap Sciences
Hangar 20 - Quai de Bacalan
Tél. : 05 56 01 07 07 Open from Tuesday to Friday from 2 pm to 6 pm
Saturdays and Sundays from 2 pm to 7 pm.
contact@cap-sciences.net www.cap-sciences.net
Exhibits and demonstrations open to all.
Discovery of scientific phenomena, technological principles, industrialknowledges....

Th. Sanson Mairie de Bordeaux

Base Sous Marine
Boulevard Alfred Daney
Tél : 05 56 11 11 50
2 pm -6pm Closed Mondays and public holidays

Temporary exhibitions

Croiseur Colbert
opposite 60 Quai des Chartrons
Tél.: 05 56 44 96 11
Open every day from 10 am to 6 pm from the 1st of April to the 31st of October, and open every day except Mondays Tuesdays, Christmas Day and New Year's Day from 10 am to 5 pm from the 1st of November to the 31st of March.

Discover what life was like aboard a large cruiser, from the engine rooms to the bridge. Exhibitions on naval history and techniques.

Galerie des Beaux-Arts
Place du colonel Raynal
Tél. : 05 56 96 51 60
11am.-6 pm
Closed Tuesdays and public holidays

Temporary exhibitions

FINDING YOUR WAY ABOUT